# THE GREATEST DECEPTION

# THE GREATEST CELESTIAL DECEPTION

## about the bright morning star

# Sam Oputa

The Greatest Celestial Deception

Sam Oputa, Copyright © 2018

ALL RIGHTS RESERVED

The author is hereby established as the sole holder of the copyright.

ISBN: 1719573352

ISBN 13: 9781719573351

## Table of Contents

About the Author ..................................................................v

Preface..................................................................................vi

Chapter One      Introduction................................................12

Chapter Two      Heard the Fat Lies?....................................16

Chapter Three      Be Inquisitive .........................................24

Chapter Four Children of the Sun & the Stars .......................30

Chapter Five  Contrasting the Syncretism of the Gods .........64

Chapter Six      Solstices ....................................................69

Chapter Seven   The Guide to the Sons of the Sun...............72

Chapter Eight Why Easter Is Celebrated in the Spring ..........78

Chapter Nine      Cross of the Zodiac, Cross of the Disciples ..80

Chapter Ten      Individualizing the Sun and the Stars & Destroying Fake Legacies ......................................................86

Chapter Eleven   Omnipresence of Solar Gods......................94

Chapter Twelve  The Ages & the End of the World...............97

Chapter Thirteen   They Made Fools of Us ..........................104

Chapter Fourteen   Historical or Historicized Jesus.............108

Chapter Fifteen  Conclusion—Behold the Light of the World ..................................................................................120

Bibliography ........................................................................145

# About the Author

Raised in an environment where there was no religion, and even where there were pockets of it, religion was never forced. No one cared what you practiced.

Sam Oputa was fascinated by religion and how it was subtly used to manipulate our thought processes. Though curious about religions, Sam's deep interest lies in spirituality.

Sam attended Baruch College of the City University of New York. He is also the author of *God Is Not Enough, Messiah Needed; Faith or Reason, All The God We Cannot See,* and *Why Was Man Created?*

Other books include *Akashic Records or Free Will: Finding Your Calling, Immaterial Existence, Hidden Barriers in The Set Up,* and *Journey of the Soul.*

# Preface

Long ago, before we were born, greedy but powerful people had discovered that with misinformation running rampant, the truth could not be protected.

Such a scenario gives cover to those seeking economic and political dominance. They have mustered the gall to dress their fearmongering, greed, deceit, and groveling under the cloak of religion. Soon, they realized that with religion, they could create a mask of lies. And they did and were very successful at it.

They never anticipated that someday, people like Robert G. Ingersoll (1833–1899) would wake up to learn about religion and conclude that "Religion can never reform mankind because religion is slavery."

And even before that, another well-known, Thomas Paine (1737–1809), concluded that: ". . . I do not believe in the creed professed by the Jewish Church, by the Roman Church, by the Greek Church, by the Turkish Church, by the Protestant Church, nor by any church that

I know of. My own mind is my church. Human nature is not of itself vicious."

And that is if you are assigning goodness and good deeds to and by the instructions of religions. For if you have your mind full of logic and reason, the need for religion as a guide to doing right and abstaining from bad is unnecessary.

Our minds are already set to decipher good from bad. We all learn these things by the intellect.

So, sometimes you must be diligent as well as inquisitive to bring the truth to light. People must not be allowed to change historical facts to empower their grip on social, economic, or political standing in society.

Even at this hour, the spread of false information as propaganda is rampant and directly aimed at those who are most vulnerable.

Fear, like love, is an emotional feeling. It is one of our animal instincts. Once you catch it, it is difficult to shed because it becomes one of your intellects. You can, however, defeat fear with the truth—the scientific facts.

The truth is available only to those who dig for it. With the truth, you then can circumvent fear. Just like Daniel J. Boorstin said: "The greatest obstacle to discovery is not ignorance—it is the illusion of knowledge."

# The Greatest Celestial Deception

Daniel J. Boorstin went on to equivocate that: "Education is learning what you didn't even know you didn't."

And, hopefully, with courage, you can begin to question whatever you have been taught as religion and history and other related subjects.

As you well know, histories, like religions, are written by the victor for the vanquished to assimilate.

Those that use fear as a weapon against you don't respect you; they despise you and expect nothing good from you. In fact, they expect the worst from you. Any attempt by you to impress them leads to an escalation of your very fears.

The way it was back then, and even now, the greedy and powerful learned how to use fear as a weapon. The lesson they learned and tried to implement was/is that if they are greedy and their pockets deep enough and your mind dull enough to succumb to fear, it does not matter that they are wrong.

They already know that sooner or later, you would be subdued because your consciousness is already dull enough.

When you start to question what you have been made to accept as the truth, you would have abruptly discovered that those techniques back then no longer have a grip on your thought processes.

# The Greatest Celestial Deception

The new perspective must be that if you question the "truth" enough—relearn the newly found truth enough—the greedy feeders of fear will start to lose. Their techniques to inflict fear will no longer frighten. You start to see the techniques for what they are, and their grip on you starts to loosen. The way I thought you and I must see it is: Succumbing to fear is like we are TVs and radios being muted by those that perpetrate fear.

You ultimately start to gain, and they start to lose when you question the false but naïvely accepted teachings.

Ultimately, nothing limits you like your fears, and your fears shape your beliefs and behavior. Nothing controls you but your beliefs; and finally, nothing binds you and makes you who you are except your thoughts—your thoughts that are, of course, shaped—from a combination of intellects.

# The Greatest Celestial Deception

# Chapter One
# Introduction

In *The Greatest Celestial Deception*, we take you on a profound journey into the heart of ancient mind-set and practices, revealing a breathtaking, hidden reality that will transform your life forever and in many ways. Far from offering simple interpretations, platitudes, and general principles, *The Greatest Celestial Deception* immerses you into the surprisingly archaic practices in the world of the ancients of various ages while using modern knowledge as a guide. While presenting you with all the incredible evidence to support this, you will discover for yourself that modernity has not put a dent in how or what the ancients worshipped or religious practices of modern people.

I have heard many people say: "I cannot be duped by anyone or any group." Well, buckle your seat belt for this ride. You are about to discover that you *are* being duped already.

After reading this, you may experience one or a combination of feelings—of anger, happiness, relief, surprise, cheated, deceived, shocked, shame, or just a simple "I told you so" moment. I hope depression is not one of them and does not set in.

If a Christian reads this, s/he will be very curious at the beginning of the book, very disappointed at the end, and probably get very depressed later.

If an Atheist reads this, I bet s/he would simply say: "I told you so."

If a Deist comes across this book, s/he may likely buy it for gifting.

Adherents of Judaism would likely look you in the eyes and say: "Now, you know. We told you He was no Messiah, but you did your thing anyway."

Yet, Animists, worldwide, would shake their heads in disbelief at human ignorance/stupidity in a rush to learn "modern" accepted practices. They will tell you: "That is why we don't do those modern holy practices."

I feel the deepest for the Christian. All those years of adhering to those beliefs now amount to nothingness. All those teachings, they exclaim, were purposeful disinformation.

All those restrictions to curb behaviors . . . All the misery in fasting and abstinence from "worldly" pleasures . . . All the times spent on their knees praying for those things and receiving no answers . . .

The worst being the times spent proselytizing to others, some of whom despised them.

And now, you find this?

This must be devastatingly stressful and excruciating. I feel you. I have always wondered why sanctioned slavery practice existed, and why it lasted so long. The slaves too were taught to serve their masters because their reward was "in heaven." I have reasoned that anyone—let alone a God—with even an iota of the milk of human kindness cannot let this be.

Any resistance to the master was a sin, punishable now and in the afterlife with misery for eternity. That should have been a clue that religion is evil, but the inventors were clever, cunning, and manipulative.

They maneuvered and closed any emerging loophole. Believers still do this, even up to this day. They defend the indefensible not realizing how unrealistic, unreasonable, and illogical they sound.

They have been taught to believe that they are wise, and you, the unwise one. They have their memorized battle cries which are the numerous verses in their books they point to, to prove that you are not as smart as they are.

I must give it to them—the crafters of the stories. They were geniuses who took the art of deception to the highest mountains, a height very difficult to reach in ancient times.

Perhaps I should feel more for those slaves who were promised heaven and strived for it, or must I be glad for those slaves who revolted and paid the ultimate price, not caring whether they would inherit hell?

The good news is: We now know what heaven and hell are, and no one is, thankfully, going to hell.

Jobs come and go, riches are made, and riches are lost. Empires rise and fall, just like emperors rise and their reigns come to an end.

Physical beauty fades.

Markets rise and fall.

Close relationships and marriages can end, but the truth—facts—will stand the test of time.

This book is not to ridicule you and your religion, or any religion, for that matter; it is about illuminating a room—not necessarily a dark one—but the room of the mind. If your mind deems it fit and right to allow such illumination, then my purpose on earth has just inched a few steps upward.

Therefore, dig in to find out what all this is about.

# Chapter Two    Heard the Fat Lies?

Some things we thought we knew about human history will have to be rewritten for it even to start to make any sense today. This is because some of the things we read are simply . . . Lies intended for misinformation, disinformation, an exercise pursuant to implanting ignorance, fear, and much more. It is time to shine some light on them. Thinking writers present and beyond, like Thomas Paine, had put a finger on religion and observed that:

*The Christian religion is a parody on the worship of the Sun, in which they put a man whom they call Christ, in the place of the Sun, and pay him the same adoration which was originally paid to the Sun.*

Though I have picked Christianity as a point of focus, other religions have suffered the same manipulations.

The writers of the books of the Bible and those that gathered at the Councils of Nicaea understood even at those times that most readers of the books will miss the trees for the forest.

The borrowed plot lines were preordained—so they make the Bible seem to profess. The calibration was measured to explode and splash fear in the minds of the readers.

The overarching intent being to never bore your mind while nudging you to that perimeter where they want you—in the circle of fear.

Among other methods, they employed the use of sophisticated word articulation and artistry to craft their messages to hide the real purpose and intent which, of course, is fear.

But that kind of craftiness was almost always designed to sell an agenda . . . the agenda of fear. With such maneuverings, there goes the distinction between truth and an alternative truth, religion and con artistry. The latter does everything and anything to deceive to sell false propaganda. Such con artistry becomes a perfected behavior.

Religion thrives on inflicting and propagating the maximum fear. Religion has perfected fear to a science. As an art too, the communications were scribbled and packaged at delivering the maximum punch of fear.

# The Greatest Celestial Deception

The attempt to subjugate followers and nonbelievers alike has been set in motion from that time.

The degree you as an individual can control any fear is what makes you act in ways between sanity and insanity.

Perpetrators of fear, we very well know, dehumanize their victims. Sometimes perpetrators use fear in hopes of attaining a variety of set objectives.

Some can manage fear very well up to where they package and sell it. Whether you will agree you have bought into fear is debatable. In most instances, those who choose fear as a weapon are far too gone in their rabid hatred of those they despise—a group or enemy in their society.

When they come to their senses, if they ever do, they realize that they were no heroes or nationalists of their tribe or group or association. They were simply killers on the rampage to attain some greedy goals. The history of religion contains the use of force and death as punishment for nonbelievers and sinners.

By the time reason, once again, takes control of their being, the damage has already been inflicted, histories obliterated, humans savaged, and the earth we have will have been scorched beyond recognition.

Most people on earth today have bought into fear, and they don't know it. It does not matter where you live; you live under some fears. Sometimes we live under the fear of our societal laws. However, the fear of our laws is not under discussion here.

If you live by religion, you have signed a mortgage—a buy into fear. Fear has been packaged and sold to you. And you bought it . . . hook, line, and sinker.

Religion has been used to dehumanize despised peoples. When people are dehumanized, it becomes very easy to exterminate them. It is simple logic. Sometimes, it is simply explained away in the idiom:

*Give a dog a bad name to kill it.*

Every country has their dehumanized people—those people they give a bad name. Usually, they are the dregs of society. They are dregs because societies put them there.

When you exhaustively and thoughtfully explore the minds of those who weaponize fear, you would find that such peoples or institutions have concluded that they are incapable of appreciating the humanity of others.

Religion was one of the easiest and earliest means to *de-Soul*—so to speak—and dehumanize certain categories of people. Religion (the three Abrahamic ones) has not laid any foundation for credibility. The only given for all three is the ability to create fear.

Depending on the philosophical system, a soul can either be immortal or mortal, but there are speculations that the church did nothing while black people were being carted away and sold as slaves because black people had *no* souls.

They were equated to or less than animals. Even to this day, some groups of people are compared to or referred to as "animals" and thereby treated as such. As an example, if you have access to Google, you can type in any race/color of people (that you may or may not have despised) and associate it with these words: *as animals*. You will be shocked at the amount of denigration and dehumanization that exists everywhere.

Whether such speculations have the truth is not the issue. The issue was that the church wavered for too long, succumbing time after time to the caprices of the political and economic standings of the time.

Christianity was also used to defend slavery. The facts are there for you to find and read. Other religions were culpable too and it is one of the reasons you must view religion—not cultures—with suspicion.

In America, slavery was justified and condemned by both sides taking their cues from the Bible. According to one side, the story of Ham in the Bible was a direct order from Noah's mouth to God's ears.

They narrate the Bible's tale of Ham—one of the sons of Noah—who they claim was accursed to serve his brothers as a slave—a total misinterpretation of the Bible. Even if it was not a misinterpretation, the Bible, however, detailed how the market for slavery should be conducted. In other words, sanctioning the practice.

There are many narratives and spin to Ham's curse, but I like the description where Ham suddenly became a representation of black and servitude. In a *New York Times* narrative titled "From Noah's Curse to Slavery's Rationale," we read, in part

> *... In the biblical account, Noah and his family are not described in racial terms. But as the story echoed through the centuries and around the world, variously interpreted by Islamic, Christian and Jewish scholars, Ham came to be widely portrayed as black; blackness, servitude and the idea of racial hierarchy became inextricably linked.*
>
> *By the 19th century, many historians agree, the belief that African-Americans were descendants of Ham was a primary justification for slavery among Southern Christians ...*

In appreciating the lack of humanity of others, there was no thinking twice before Africans were displayed in American and European zoos to be gawked at in the recent past of the early 1900s. We can only imagine the level of inhumanity years ago.

Our leaders use fear as an incentive or even deterrent. The biblical God used fear to control the Israelites. Our lives are controlled with and by fear. Fears of war, of hunger, of jail, etc., have been weaponized for control.

Perhaps the biggest fear weaponized is that of death. Heaven and hell were manufactured. Death was instituted and later osmosed into all our systems and institutions to scare the crap out of you.

The world of today, like yesterday, is/was often inhabited by fear, so much so, that national policies are dictated by fear.

Years ago, oligarchs and their enforcers were regularly and intentionally cooking up ever-malleable and watered-down truths to sow fear, not caring who or what is destroyed as they pursued those goals.

Today, lies have metamorphosed into alternative truths as if a truth of 2+2 can be something else other than 4. Ideally, truth should be an easy term to define because the truth is fact. Fact is a provable data you can rely on today or tomorrow. It stands the test of time. Up is up while down is down. Up is never down. Today, however, alternative truths have become the framework on which lies and fear are built.

Today, counterfeit truths are being perpetuated by political parties and allies supported by financial benefactors, disseminated by opportunistic partisan media houses, and blessed by a faction of the clergy.

You will soon see that you have been living the fear all your life and you never knew it because you have accepted and normalized the lies.

For any humanity-thinking person, to dismiss weaponized fear in whatever form—even as the Bible—as an anomaly, is to miss the forest for the trees.

Are you scared yet? It is not too early to batten down the hatches.

# Chapter Three  Be Inquisitive

An American president once said, "We have nothing to fear but fear itself." He knew and understood what a weapon fear is.

In fact, powerfully greedy leaders who know how to weaponize fear have used fear to rise to the top. History is available to pinpoint such leaders.

Even if we were born in ignorance, education could help to quench the flames of fear and thus open our eyes to questioning fears.

"We are all born ignorant, but one must work hard to remain stupid." That was a quote ascribed to a president of the United States of America by Benjamin Franklin.

The Founding Fathers of today's America seemed to have known what leads to greater ignorance and timidity, and they sought to keep it at arm's length. They systematically kept religion at bay.

In fact, the Founders were very suspicious of religion, which in their time would have been Judaism, Islam, but mostly Christianity—the same three Abrahamic religions mentioned earlier. They separated religions from affairs of State.

They sought intelligent voices of reason guided by truth and freedoms—the foundation of America's democracy—without which the country, any country, has nothing.

You may have heard some persons refer to the United States as a "Christian nation." They don't know any better.

Perhaps, that was the history they have been fed in our schools, and they are seriously working very hard to make that assertion the truth.

The truth is that America is *not* a Christian nation.

The Founders were smart men who knew better. America is a nation founded on the belief that all people have religious freedom, and that includes having no religion at all.

The moment you take an audit of the education you were exposed to in schools, it does not take long before you start to document some of the inadequacies and inaccuracies, in your mind, of what has been fed to you as education.

## The Greatest Celestial Deception

You begin to realize that you learned what was selected and decided for you, and even at that, what you learned was full of untruths, unnecessary propaganda, and sometimes, outright disinformation.

You begin to ask questions like: Why? There is a feeling that if they remove all the false information, there will be no story to tell. You start to notice and perhaps, understand that some of the stories are told from the point of strength—not necessarily from the point of truth.

When you read one of any history books for the first time, you are very likely to believe the story even if the story has been salted and peppered with untruths. The reader is not to blame. The blame should be on the writer, but when you read the same book or other history books and keep assimilating untruths every time, perhaps the blame must be on you.

One of the bestselling and most read books—the Bible—has been read over and over. With so many people who had read the Bible for hundreds of times and much more without a bat of the eyelid as you accept the gospels as truths, the blame is on you.

You need to ask questions . . . and more questions.

There are some truths if you are nearly as inquisitive. Every writing by anyone, including this one, is from a perspective. Find what that perspective is, and you might get the purpose for such writing, whether the writing is seeking truth or purposefully planting falsehoods.

When the Bible writers wrote to inform its readers that the world was created in 6 days, why would that not raise red flags immediately? It can be one of these intentions: Either the writers were deluded, or the intent was to misinform, disinform, or to wow its readers. If the readers were wowed in ancient times, at least they had some excuses.

What are *our* excuses today?

When you and I were growing up, we were told what and how to think. We were told what to eat. We were told how to behave, and mostly, we behaved like those who had colonized us.

Our education was doctored. The history we were taught had nothing to do with the forefathers of the students.

In fact, monuments and landmarks that the forefathers have confirmed their existence from time immemorial, we are now told were discovered by some expedition carried out by sailors foreign to the lands.

The education was such that history recounts the land that is today Mesoamerica, and the extending areas as having been discovered by a sailor/explorer.

The whole history is tainted and feigned. The history was not anything about truth and education anymore. It is about disinformation, subjugation, and greed.

If the intent was greed and subjugation, both have permeated all aspects of life in areas of history and especially religion. If what we now know is miseducation of the people, what events of history may have been changed for a further perfect miseducation of the people?

The more you question and investigate what we have been told and taught as truths, you begin to find that we have all been lied to by all the established institutions.

We have been lied to so much that one begins to wonder if the church teachings are free from untruths. On a closer look, you begin to discover that those who prepped our school syllabuses were the same who doctored what we are taught or not taught.

You discover that those who gave us our institutions of governments, history, laws, wars, etc., were the same class of people who gave us our religion. They still are the controllers of the major worldwide markets, banks, and religions.

Findings are showing that religious institutions are at the bottom of manipulated institutions. They messed with religions so much so, it is turning out to be all lies. Lies! Lies!! Lies everywhere!!!

This is not to malign any religion or the one you belong to or believe in. That you "believe" is all the evidence you need to know that you do not know anything about what you believe in. To believe does not equal truth or fact.

Where there is evidence to point to the truth, you do not need to "believe" to know. You know because the evidence that point to the truth is available for scrutiny.

To believe is another acronym for faith, a deceitful word used to con people.

God/Consciousness is neither Jewish nor Christian. Consciousness did not create religion. Religion was an invention by men for subjugation purposes.

The purpose of this work, therefore, is to begin at the beginning to find how they managed to feed such religious lies to the people for such a very long time.

We should not deny people's experiences. But, we can deny their interpretations of their experiences.

# Chapter Four Children of the Sun & the Stars

1. Zephaniah 1:5 (NRSV):

those who bow down on the roofs to the host of the heavens;
those who bow down and swear to the LORD, but also swear by Milcom;

2. Deuteronomy 17:3 (NRSV)

by going to serve other gods and worshiping them—whether the sun or the moon or any of the host of heaven, which I have forbidden—

3. Deuteronomy 4:19 (NRSV):

And when you look up to the heavens and see the sun, the moon, and the stars, all the host of heaven, do not be led astray and bow down to them and serve them, things that the LORD your God has allotted to all the peoples everywhere under heaven.

4. Exodus 20:3–4 (NRSV)

³ you shall have no other gods before me.

⁴ You shall not make for yourself an idol, whether in the form of anything that is in heaven above, or that is on the earth beneath, or that is in the water under the earth.

There is not even a single difference in all the above quotes. They were all speaking to the same matter and, unbelievably, the same truth.

Are you beginning to observe the disintegration of religious books put together, not minding the type of allegories used and the contradictions, misinformation, and most importantly, disinformation?

If anything, these quotes above must remind you or at least make you aware that that the biblical God—Yahweh—is different from the New Testament's Son of God. If, like me, you ask, which is the real God?—you won't be alone.

*Who/which God?* I have almost always asked. Do not get confused. Indeed, those quotes above confirms the worship of other gods—the moon, the stars, and especially the sun.

Such practice is known as astrolatry.

There is another term—*astrotheology*. The word astrotheology comes from the Greek word *Astron* meaning star. Astrotheology is used to describe a religious system based on the observation of the heavens.

Astrotheology gives an insight, perhaps a system, to decoding the Bible. For example, let us look at a Bible verse and consider how you would interpret the same verse after you finish reading this book. Here is the verse: John 8:12 (NRSV):

> *Again Jesus spoke to them, saying, "I am the light of the world. Whoever follows me will never walk in darkness but will have the light of life."*

That Jesus spoke to them is because of anthropomorphism—the attribution of human traits, intention, or emotions to nonhuman entities.

The explanation believers give is that their religion is not a worship of the stars or the sun, but the stars are the proof of God's glory. They scare you, as always, with the threat of hell if you insist upon inquiries. They tell you that any attempt at pointing out the allegories in their books amounts to blasphemy. They argue that any attempt to deny Jesus Christ by astrotheology is abominable.

Unfortunately, astrotheology cannot deny Jesus Christ; it only explains and confirms it. There was/is nothing blasphemous or untruthful about astrotheology. It simply helps to point you in the right direction.

What then is astrotheology? It is a system based on the observation of celestial bodies.

With that said, let us then contrast a few of the solar gods that happen to be in the celestial heavens. But, we must start with Jesus because Jesus is the "Light of the World."

The following is an in-depth analysis based on research and understanding. It is also based on our progress in the areas of astronomy and astrology. Modern knowledge and ancient evidence of astrolatry practices were an invaluable guide.

## The Lord Jesus

Jesus was the most recent and most popular of all the heavenly messiahs. There are similarities between Jesus Christ and other celestial deities like Horus, Mithras, Vishnu, Attis, Dionysius, and many others . . . too many to mention here. One thing must be said here, though. And that is, these messiahs were born out of the celestial worship.

Have you heard the saying "before Abraham was born, I am"? While growing up, the colloquial version used to be "before Moses was born, I was." If you have not heard this saying, John 8:58 (NIV) would help here.

*"Very truly I tell you," Jesus answered, "before Abraham was born, **I** am!"*

By the way, Abraham lived about 400 years before Moses was born.

Do you really understand the intent and meaning of this saying? Not many do. I too did not fully understand it until recently, and it was by chance.

The Greatest Celestial Deception

All "Jesus Christ" was saying was that He was there in the beginning.

Is this true? Do not jump to conclusions because the answer is what this book is all about. For all the story about Jesus, below are the takeaways.

Jesus had a virgin birth—Holy Conception.

Jesus Christ was born allegedly on Christmas Day—the 25th of December.

He died. And most importantly, on the 3rd day, He arose from death.

The above events are very important to believers because these events are the framework on which Christianity was founded.

He was/is as is claimed and truly too, the light of the world. He is: The light.

Here is Jesus' story.

On one 25th day of December about 2,000 years ago, an angel who is named Gabriel appeared to a young woman—Mary—the Virgin. By all accounts and from histories, 2,000 years ago is very recent in human existence. Angel Gabriel announced to the Virgin that she would have a son—Jesus—who would be the Son of God.

The news was, of course, confusing and shocking for the young woman who, in this dilemma, inquired how this can be when there was no man to do the needed biological deed for conception to occur.

Mary was betrothed to Joseph, her husband-to-be. As the story goes, Joseph and Mary lived in Nazareth, but they must travel to another city—Bethlehem—to register for a census as ordered by a Roman emperor. The emperor's name the story asserts was Augustus Caesar.

History confirms the existence of Augustus Caesar. According to the narrative, both towns of Bethlehem and Nazareth were located on earth in the area presently referred to as Israel. Let us take the story from its source—the Bible.

The book of Matthew 1:18–25 (KJV) narrates it like this:

*[18] Now the birth of Jesus Christ was on this wise: When as his mother Mary was espoused to Joseph, before they came together, she was found with child of the Holy Ghost.*

*[19] Then Joseph her husband, being a just man, and not willing to make her a public example, was minded to put her away privily.*

*[20] But while he thought on these things, behold, the angel of the LORD appeared unto him in a dream, saying, Joseph, thou son of David, fear not to take unto thee*

*Mary thy wife: for that which is conceived in her is of the Holy Ghost.*

*²¹ And she shall bring forth a son, and thou shalt call his name JESUS: for he shall save his people from their sins.*

*²² Now all this was done, that it might be fulfilled which was spoken of the Lord by the prophet, saying,*

*²³ Behold, a virgin shall be with child, and shall bring forth a son, and they shall call his name Emmanuel, which being interpreted is, God with us.*

*²⁴ Then Joseph being raised from sleep did as the angel of the Lord had bidden him, and took unto him his wife:*

*²⁵ And knew her not till she had brought forth her firstborn son: and he called his name JESUS.*

Also, the Book of Luke 1:26–35 narrates the same story:

*²⁶ And in the sixth month the angel Gabriel was sent from God unto a city of Galilee, named Nazareth,*

*²⁷ To a virgin espoused to a man whose name was Joseph, of the house of David; and the virgin's name was Mary.*

*²⁸ And the angel came in unto her, and said, Hail, thou that art highly favoured, the Lord is with thee: blessed art thou among women.*

*²⁹ And when she saw him, she was troubled at his saying, and cast in her mind what manner of salutation this should be.*

*³⁰ And the angel said unto her, Fear not, Mary: for thou hast found favour with God.*

*³¹ And, behold, thou shalt conceive in thy womb, and bring forth a son, and shalt call his name JESUS.*

*³² He shall be great, and shall be called the Son of the Highest: and the Lord God shall give unto him the throne of his father David:*

*³³ And he shall reign over the house of Jacob for ever; and of his kingdom there shall be no end.*

*³⁴ Then said Mary unto the angel, How shall this be, seeing I know not a man?*

*³⁵ And the angel answered and said unto her, The Holy Ghost shall come upon thee, and the power of the Highest shall overshadow thee: therefore also that holy thing which shall be born of thee shall be called the Son of God.*

The Greatest Celestial Deception

This is the story of the virgin birth. A virgin birth is the belief that someone was conceived in the womb of their mother by divine intervention through the Holy Spirit of the Trinity without the input of a human father.

The conception and birth happened while the mother was still a virgin. The New Testament references of the story are Matthew 1:18–25 and Luke 1:26–38.

Christians are quick to reference and follow the prophetic message in Isaiah 7:14 (NRSV)

*Therefore the Lord himself will give you a sign. Look, the young woman is with child and shall bear a son and shall name him Immanuel.*

The theme of this message is, however, not expressly mentioned elsewhere in the Christian scriptures.

Recent scholarly findings indicate that the doctrine of the virgin birth rests very heavily on ancient Egyptian historical foundation. One shocking find is that Muslims also believe in the virgin birth of Jesus.

Jesus is therefore referred to as:

The Lamb of God

The Lion of Judah

The Almighty

The Alpha and Omega

The Giver of Life

# The Greatest Celestial Deception

The Son of God

The Light of the World

The Bright Morning Star

What else do you perceive to be the light of the world? It is important to think out of the box here. Did you hazard a guess?

As a Christian, you are likely to believe that the concept of a virgin birth first happened with the story and birth of Jesus. That is not so. The concept has been in the books many thousands of years before it was *copied*.

The concept has been in visual forms on the walls of ancient Egyptian buildings and in the books of the pharaohs, and their concept is much older than what we have been led to accept and believe. You'd be shocked to learn that the virgin birth is a concept copied not only by Christianity but various religions worldwide.

Religions have made falsehoods true. Religions have blended true myths to serve a purpose for the leaders of that time. Whether the intent was a genuine attempt to shape human behavior or an intent to inflict the wrath of a few controlling ruling cabals is not known precisely, but if we understand human behavior, we can project that religion was invented and designed for control.

It is that simple and easily fathomable too. It is disheartening that many people have gone to their graves believing what they believe—a lie. Millions of people have believed in teachings that were intended for disinformation. They believed because, in the eyes of the innocent, the teachings appear to be convincing and true. If you don't believe their teachings, they convince you that there is a thing called faith. When that fails, they describe your culture and practices as paganism and Satanism. They make you feel less of a human and even threaten your well-being and life. They are succeeding, especially with the promise of heaven or hell in an afterlife as your two choices.

Many people at that time fell for false propaganda, perhaps because they were naïve and could not decipher that certain sections of society feel they can feed us baloney, and some of us would consider it a sandwich and eat it up.

A little reason and logic can crack many a falsehood. But some of us don't take time to allow a little bit of reason to take place. If the ancients were naïve—being innocent, uninformed, misinformed, and incapable of discernment—with all the intelligence available at our fingertips today, we can't claim to be stupid. Stupidity becomes a choice.

Even leaders in today's world who understand the use of propaganda rise to prominent public office positions using such rabble-rousing, imbecilic, false, and trouble-creating messages to reach many people.

Thanks to Consciousness, it does not matter what you believe in. It does matter, though, what you believe in when it affects your spending patterns in associations or groups, especially when having the right information would have stopped disastrously wealth-draining spending.

When I wrote the lines below in the book *Akashic Records or Free Will: Finding Your Calling*, little did I know that I just laid the foundation for this book you are reading now. When I started receiving requests to expand on these paragraphs, I knew something was up and knew I must comply. I had to answer to my readers even if it meant distant travels to different places seeking knowledge.

Here are the lines from page 1:

*Have you ever heard anyone say, "It's all in the stars"? At least there is one star we have come to know very well. You see it every morning and see it disappear in the evenings. When it disappears, you know it is time to conclude the day's business. We use it to measure time, days, months, and years. Without it, the crops, and indeed, humans, cannot survive. It is so well known and important to our daily lives, some of our forefathers thought they might as well deify it. The mythology of the Aten—the radiant disk—the sun, is not only unique in Egyptian history, but is also one of the most complex and controversial aspects of Ancient Egypt's new one religion. The ancient Egyptian name for the disk of the sun was Aten, which is first evidenced during the reign of Akhenaten. In stories, all credit for the actual recognition of the Sun deity Aten is credited to Amenhotep IV, who also is referred to as Akhenaten, Pharaoh King of Egypt.*

*If you really dig very deep, you will find the finger rays of the sun in modern-day popular religions. The sun and some other celestial stars have a clear and apparent material effect on our planetary system and especially our planet—Earth. The effect of the sun on earthly beings needs no explanation. The sun through the aid and the providence of the Universal Intelligence impacts the Earth and all earthly beings in no small way. Without the light and heat of the sun, perhaps all the earthly creatures would be nonexistent.*

Let us expand on the disk of the sun here. Aten was the disk of the sun in ancient Egyptian mythology. It was also originally an aspect of the god Ra.

Let it not be lost on you that the worship of the sun god was the first attempt at monotheism. Aten was a being who represented the god and/or the spirit of the sun (rays) and the actual solar disk. The symbol for its depiction was a disk with rays stretching/radiating down to earth.

In the depiction are human hands stretched out to grab the rays of the sun, and at the same time, the hands extended to hand over the ankh to the pharaoh.

# The Greatest Celestial Deception

The 18th-dynasty Pharaoh Akhenaten forbade the worship of many gods. This was a very radical departure from the centuries of Egyptian practices. It was Akhenaten who decreed that the name Aten was no longer to be depicted by the hieroglyphic language of writing—the use of a solar disc emitting sunrays—instead, the king ordered that the Aten be spelled out phonetically.

Pharaoh Akhenaton's religious reforms which would be essentially discarded because they were regarded as heretical, have been described by some scholars as the beginning of a monotheistic culture.

In some sort of psalmlike poem—Great Hymn to the Aten—Akhenaten poured encomiums on Aten as the Creator, Giver of Life, and Nurturing Spirit of the World. Aten does not have a creation myth, but Aten has mentions in the Egyptian Book of the Dead.

The sun is a star, just like other stars you see in the sky in the night. The sun, however, looks brighter because of its proximity to Earth. The sun is 8 minutes in light-years away from Earth, whereas other faint distant stars we see in the night are many light-years away.

The sun is classified as a G2-type star closest to Earth. There are many G2-type stars and Earth's sun is just one among billions of stars that orbit the center of our galaxy. The sun emits energized particles that make the solar wind. This energy strikes the earth as sun rays.

The earth warms up, our weather fluctuates, and so provides energy for life. You can understand now why our forefathers refer to the sun as the "giver of life." Do you blame them?

Without going too much into the history of ancient Egypt, one take-out from this short mention of Akhenaten and the Aten (Aton) was the beginning in the attempt to impose a monotheistic cultural practice.

Most readers and scholars of history have been conditioned to accept that this attempt was a colossal failure because, according to history, such practices were reversed immediately by succeeding pharaohs after the death of Akhenaten.

Did such practice fail completely as history was written to make us believe?

We shall answer this question in later pages, and the answer will shock you to the core of your belief system. You will come to understand that what had been packaged as religions and sold to you as best practices were nothing new but part of a plagiarized version of ancient Egypt's Book of the Dead.

It was a regurgitation of cultural practices in Africa that had been "championed" or "koshered," for lack of a better adjective, by powers that be as a tool to control their subjects.

In Africa, it was just a cultural practice, but in the hand of the Greeks and Romans, it became a practice that must be weaponized to instill fear. The practice became a weapon by which many became conditioned to servitude. The practice would then be preached and enforced worldwide.

One little hint: Ever notice a halo on a religious motif? Halo demonstrates light. It is the furtherance of the sun disk—the Aten disk. The story of the sun continues as we discuss the god Ra.

## The Sun: Ra

To the ancient peoples that occupied the continent, now referred to as Africa, and especially for ancient Egyptians, the sun represented light, warmth, and growth. The sun—Ra, is regarded as the enabler of life on earth.

Ra was the god of the sun and creation. Don't be confused if you notice that this god is also called Amen-Re. The sun disk was observed as the body or the all-seeing eye of Ra.

It will be helpful if the reader sees the allegory in these stories. In this instance, one must understand the use of expressions by means of symbolic fictional figures to represent a certain star as a deity. You can therefore see why the sun deity is very important as it rules over the "universe" (this planetary system) and all that is in it.

The sun god was the light of the world, the giver of life, the reason our crops grow, and the usher of happiness—here on earth and in the afterlife.

As with many worshipped deities at the time, Ra's identity was often combined with other gods to form an interconnection between gods. As you may have observed, later "modern" religions would take to same practices to assimilate other gods.

It is important to point out here that this practice of identity combination led to a later Egyptian dynastic time where the sun deity metamorphosed from Ra to Ra-Horakhty—a combination of Ra and Horus.

Ra is simply the sun—the Sun God. Be that as it were, the takeout on Ra is to show the roles stars have played and continue to play in our so-called modern religions. This is a very important take, and you will remember this related importance in later chapters.

Another takeaway is reincarnation/resurrection of a god in their children. By this, it means that the father is same as the son—the son being inside the father as the father is inside the son. This concept—syncretism—would be borrowed, applied, and noticeable in major religions today. But, they won't tell us. Maybe, they too, do not get it.

Even now, you may notice many a winner on the field of play, even in the Olympics, look up to heaven, while making the sign of the cross, as if to say thank you to someone or something up there in the skies. It is a borrowed behavior from our forefathers thanking the stars for a good harvest. Who were they supplicating to in the skies?

## The Egyptian God Osiris

Osiris is believed to be the reincarnate of Ra. Osiris was an Egyptian god. Osiris was described as the god of the afterlife, the dead and the underworld. This god was also described as the god in charge of transition, regeneration, and resurrection.

When a story is told, sometimes there are names and locations inserted to give it meaning. When a writer writes a story, s/he makes a plot. It is important to understand this as we read and comprehend these stories. I might be repetitive in reminding the reader that like many stories of ancient whispers, allegories are used in the description of the gods.

For example, when they looked up at the heavens, there was the constellation Leo, Taurus, and Pisces. There are also the constellations of Orion and the star Sirius.

# The Greatest Celestial Deception

Many civilizations, past and present, give a special place to the constellation of Orion before the horns of Taurus. He stands as a great hunter with his belt of three stars.

To the Egyptians, this was Osiris—the god of the afterlife.

With the great knowledge of the stars and medicine—even at that time, Imhotep was venerated by many, especially the Greeks, as the father of medicine and the ground layer of the great pyramids. He was regarded very highly and venerated as *Asclepius*—a demigod of healing.

It was said that Osiris was one of four human-shaped gods that came out of the womb of a star goddess. The three others from that star goddess were Set—the brother of Osiris, Nephthys, and Isis—the sister and wife of Osiris.

Osiris and Isis are said to be the parents of Horus. Horus, of course, was considered as Osiris's posthumously begotten son. All the pharaohs of Egypt were associated with Osiris because the tradition states that as Osiris rose from the dead, so would the kings in union with him to live forever through a process of reincarnation.

In other words, Osiris as god is the same as his son Horus. As it is said: Osiris is in Horus as Horus is in Osiris. Osiris also reincarnated in heaven as the star Orion while Isis metamorphosed in heaven as the star Sirius.

## STILL ON OSIRIS'S DEATH

If, and when, you read about Osiris, you may read that Osiris had a brother—some say an enemy . . . Set. The story goes on to say that Osiris—son of the Sun God—has a sister—Isis.

The story would explain how Set killed Osiris. The way the stories go, if you do not understand the logic, oh yes, it is logical—you are most likely to wave off the story as just a myth.

In most of my books, I always caution that mythos must not be discarded offhand. Try to understand the myth, and suddenly, there's logic in it.

Osiris as the son of the sun—Ra—or light, rises and sets. In other words, Osiris rules the daylight.

Set as night—darkness—kills the light when it appears. And Osiris as the light when it rises kills Set—the dark. So, Set rules the darkness.

This is played out on every sunrise and every sunset. The story of Osiris is an allegory. It is full of allegorical myths and metaphors too.

So, in the day, Osiris's reign is unquestioned until the evening when Set "kills" Osiris and sends him to the underworld, only to return the next morning—sunrise.

# The Greatest Celestial Deception

As an observer, I am tempted to say: The day and night are dualities of Consciousness.

If you have read any of my books, you may have noticed that I often express the importance of dualities as the only means by which Consciousness can experience its own creations.

The story is still repeated of how Osiris was murdered by his jealous brother, Set. It is said that Set killed his brother and cut and spread the body parts across the land, and Isis, the wife and sister of Osiris, found and pieced the body parts together; however, the phallus was missing.

The story went on to explain the mysterious impregnation of Isis by dead Osiris. OK. We already know that allegories served well the representations in the story.

Osiris was a god, so if his brother/enemy was able to kill him, then the brother must also be a god too. And many have perhaps, rightly or wrongly, interpreted it so.

So, the interpretation follows that Osiris is the god of the light (day), while Set, his brother, is the god of darkness (night). Here, I ask you to separate night and day and hold the night and day in separate hands.

In each hand, you add rotation and revolution of the Earth. Throw Set into the hand holding the night. And into the other hand, you throw in Osiris.

The result is: Every 12 hours, the light would kill the darkness, and/or the darkness will kill the daylight. Set was night, and Osiris was day.

This "killing" would "continue" unto eternity.

## Isis the Goddess and Mother of God

Isis is very important in the story this book is weaving. Isis was a very important goddess in ancient Egypt. She was the wife and sister of Osiris. She was the mother of the god Horus—who had a divine birth. The goddess—Isis—was introduced as one of the main characters that depicted the gods of Egypt.

She was the sister and wife who put Osiris back together after Osiris had been chopped into fourteen pieces and bore Horus. Like other gods, this goddess has also been anthropomorphized, metamorphosed, been hijacked, adopted/adapted, and/or absorbed into the mother of/virgin births, of many gods apart from Horus.

She is closely associated with the constellation Virgo. Virgo's contemporary association with attention to details, perfectionism, and perpetual devotion began in ancient times. The perfectionism was why Virgo is associated with purity and virginity.

This singular point is very important to remember considering the very many virgin births we will be discussing later in the book.

In Egyptian mythology, Virgo, who is a representation of Isis, instructed humankind on the practice of medicine, maternity, enchantments, and spells, sorcery, and matrimony, among others.

# Horus

There are some very important reasons Horus is featured in this work. One of the most important being that Horus was the first man/pharaoh conceived mysteriously through a virgin birth and was where the concept of part man, part God has its origin.

So far, we have had our narrations using allegorical symbols as representations of the stars/gods.

With Horus, the plot would have worshippers move away from the allegories. Perhaps, we can now see the gods as pharaohs. Horus was the first human pharaoh worshipped as a god.

During the Hellenic period, Horus was identified as the reincarnation of Osiris. They started to associate him as both his father and the son of his father. He was viewed as a god, like his father, Osiris.

Stop and ponder this question for a second: In what religion is the Son compared and equated to the Father? Let us even take our imagination further. Is this even possible? Of course, it is possible. If you understand reincarnation, there would be no problem here, but that is an aside.

The real exposé here is that Horus thus becomes the first demonstration or enactment of the concept of being part human, part God. He thus was both man and a god.

Thus, the mythology of the nativity became popular in the Mediterranean and formed the basis for many a mystery religion with many different solar gods.

Notwithstanding the above points, Horus was one of the most significant gods in ancient Egyptian culture. He was worshipped from the late predynastic through Greco-Roman periods.

There were, however, various forms of Horus that were recorded in ancient whispers, and these were treated as distinct gods by Egyptologists.

After analyzing the ancient whispers of Horus, you will notice that:

Horus's conception was mysterious.

His birth was accompanied by a star in the east.

He was welcomed/visited by three kings who gifted him with three special gifts. Were those kings and gifts allegories? Whether you allegorize them as kings and gifts, the bottom line is that those were allegories.

His mother was a virgin.

He was born on December 25th.

Horus was both a god and a man.

At the age of 12, he became a prodigal child teacher in the establishments—ancient Egyptian gathering places.

At age 30, he was dipped in a flowing river as in baptism by Anup the baptizer.

Horus had 12 servants/disciples that followed him all over the place.

Horus performed miracles as well, like walking on water and healing others.

He was known as the Lamb of God, the light, the truth, God's anointed Son, the good shepherd, and so many other praise names.

He raised El-azur-us from the dead.

He was betrayed and killed.

He was said to have descended into the underworld.

He rose from death on the 3rd day.

## The Greatest Celestial Deception

It was as if and reasonably so that a real forerunner for Jesus Christ was unwittingly being established.

And all the above, supposedly, happened at and around 3000 BC, a period when Jesus had not yet existed. This is not to suggest that He ever existed, but it is reasonable when He is referred to as fictional or one of those solar messiah characters. Let us consider some what-ifs here:

Assume that Horus had filed a suit in court that his identity was stolen. If you were a juror weighing the evidence as per the characteristics listed above, and if we were in a court examining those characteristics as evidence for a conviction, wouldn't you seek to convict beyond any reasonable doubt based on what has been said of Horus so far?

Would you at least consider that those characteristics were hijacked/stolen from old practices to supplement the present-day practices? Today, there is no denying which came first. There is no chicken or egg causality dilemma here.

Wouldn't you think that since one came before the other, one is original and the other a replication? One, the original; the other, fake? One, the truth, the other, make-believe?

You see, some of the critics of the history of Jesus often argue that the parallels between the ideology of Horus and that of the story of Jesus indicate that they are the same story. The later occurrence just was a repeat or a hijack from a different time.

If you think about it, you can easily conclude that one of the stories assimilated or hijacked the other. The argument that the Jesus idea failed to consider the belief in Horus is one that spans thousands of years.

There are many different versions to the solar messiahs, but aren't all the versions an attempt to further the deception?

All along, we have been guided into accepting each era of belief in Horus or its revised solar messiah equivalent, none of which they told us matched up with the accounts of Jesus.

The point is simply that the accounts for all the solar messiahs match up.

## Attis the God

Attis was the consort of Cybele in Phrygian and Greek mythology. Attis was also a Phrygian god of vegetation, and in his self-mutilation, death, and resurrection, he represents the seeds of the earth which die in winter and rise again in the spring.

Originally a deity in the region of Phrygia, the cult of Attis and Cybele eventually spread to Greece. According to this cult, the origins of Attis were linked to the figure Agdistis.

Agdistis was a deity of Greek, Roman, and Anatolian myth. Agdistis possessed both male and female sexual organs and was connected to Phrygian worship of Attis and Cybele.

Meanwhile, there were some commentaries on what modern Attis-related scholarship make of any alleged connection to any of the solar messiahs, especially Jesus Christ. There are arguments that the similarities were because of graftage from Jesus unto Attis.

Critics of these similarities say that most of the materials about Attis were brought on by people bent on discrediting Christianity. The material they get excited over was from a time mostly postdating Christianity.

They make such arguments while having selective amnesia. They conveniently forget Ra, Horus, and ancient whispers of Egyptian practices.

All the rebuttals about who grafted who, aside, below are some of the similarities with other solar messiahs.

Like Horus, like Jesus, Attis was born on the 25th of December. Lots of people are born on the 25th of December. We all understand that, but there were so many similarities shared between Horus, Jesus, and Attis.

There were so many myths that apply to the solar gods, you begin to wonder about such coincidences. It takes very little to set inquisitive and inquiring minds off.

Evidence points to all these gods having had their origin from the solar systems.

Not only was Attis born on the 25th of December by a virgin mother—Nana—Attis was also crucified and was resurrected on the 3rd day. He was considered the savior who was killed for the salvation of mankind. His body is eaten as bread by his followers while his priests were eunuchs.

*What?* you may ask, but no one is making stuff up here.

Attis was represented as a "man tied unto a tree" and at the bottom of the tree was a lamb. He was known to have gone to the underworld after he died. He was resurrected from death after three days. And that was celebrated around March 25th.

He was described as a shepherd, and like Jesus, was referred to as the "good shepherd."

Above all, Attis served as the divine Son and the Father as in part man, part God. He was referred to as the "Most High God" after resurrection.

## Krishna as the Chief Herdsman

Krishna is one of the gods so widely revered in parts of Asia. The outreach is spreading to the West and Africa now. Krishna is the most popular of all Indian divinities.

He is worshipped as the eighth incarnation of the Hindu god Vishnu. Krishna is a Supreme God as he is the second person in the Hindu Trinity.

Like the incarnate of all the other solar gods, Hindus believe Krishna lived on earth guesstimating the period as between 2nd and 3rd century BC. Some say he was born on December 25th, but there are those who question the date.

According to fact checkers, the season of birth is estimated at late August or early September when Hindus celebrate the birthday. The point here is that no one is particularly sure of the actual date.

Krishna is often represented in Indian traditions in various ways. His color is mostly represented as black or blue skin. He is often accompanied by cows symbolizing the divine herdsman—*Govinda*.

Does this remind you of yet another savior-god who is often described as a shepherd?

Earliest text depictions of Krishna as a personality can be found in the epic Mahabharata. It will interest you to know a few similarities between this god and Jesus. Make the comparisons and draw a conclusion for yourself.

Both claim that they are the resurrection. Krishna and Jesus were also remembered for withdrawing into the wilderness and fasting. Both also claimed to have existed before they were born. They claim to be divine and human and without sin.

They were both considered omniscient, omnipresent, and omnipotent. At this point, there is a temptation on my part to input opinions on omnipresence, but I will save myself that repetition of work that is already available in one my other books—*Faith or Reason.* But even then, the solar gods could be said to have omnipresence and those other characteristics associated with the god(s).

After all, the gods are solar in their origin. Our universe and our planetary system, as you already know, is much bigger than our planet, yet our only sun rubs on all the planets. If you thought there were similarities between Krishna and Jesus, wait until we compare Jesus' characteristics and those of Mithra, sometimes written as Mitra or Mithras.

## Mithra of Persia

Whether it was the Indian Mitra or the Persian Mithra, it is essentially the same solar deity representing the benefits we get from the sun. This deity even morphed as Mitu and Itu, which were derivatives of Mitu and Mitra. It was worshipped everywhere as a Hindu god in India.

Mithra is considered as the vegetation deity. Mithra or Mitra, a Sun-God, was believed to be a mediator between God and man—another way of saying—between the heavens and the Earth. It is also the belief of Hindus that Mithra—the Sun-God—was born of a virgin—Anahita.

And his symbol is the Lamb.

Without delving too much into the history of this deity, there are important facts about this god that resonate with the import of this book which is: Presenting and connecting the evidences that point to the origin of these solar messiahs as the celestial bodies of the planetary system—the sun—being at the center because its shine is beneficial a lot more.

Mithra (sometimes called Mithras) was called "the Divine Sun" or "the Unconquered Sun" around the Greco-Roman period. He was venerated as "greatest king of gods," "the mediator between heaven and earth," and as a "mighty ruler." Mithra was born on December 25 by a virgin.

He was said to have traveled far and wide with his 12 disciples. Mithra's great celebrations took place in the Winter Solstice and the Vernal Equinox—Christmas and Easter.

Mithra, like Jesus, was venerated as "the Way," "the Truth," "the Life," "the Light," "the Word," "the Son of God," and as "the Good Shepherd."

One of the symbols representing Mithra was that of "carrying a lamb on his shoulders"—the same symbol used to represent Jesus Christ.

Mithraism or Mithraic practice was a mystery religion practiced by followers of the god Mithra in the Roman Empire at about the 1st to the 4th century BCE.

Does Mithra remind you of any god yet? Does he remind you of Ra—the sun god of Egypt or Akhenaten's sun disk—Aten? Does Mithras remind you of Horus, Attila, or another of the solar gods?

If anything, Mithra, as we have already seen, makes Jesus Christ look so good like a twin.

# Chapter Five  Contrasting the Syncretism of the Gods

It will be unbelievable if you have not already made some comparisons based on the above gods and the many not-discussed ones. Be that as it were, there is one thing common to all of them—anthropomorphism—the attribution of human traits to deities.

In my book, *All The God We Cannot See*, a chapter was devoted to comparing and contrasting of mankind's and gods' behaviors and the attribution of human traits to the deities.

The attribution of human traits meant that each god could speak, could get jealous, could have a son, and could visit the iniquities of the fathers on their sons.

As part of the attribution of human traits to nonhuman deities, the deity can, therefore, write, love, hate, make agreements, and demand adulation and adoration.

At some point in the evolution of the different deities, followers must have thought: How can we make our god greater than their gods? Suddenly, syncretism became a way out. Creators of these religions, for example, at Nicaea, realized that to dodge some awkward questions and in the process attract more followers, they needed to make their god—the father and an incarnate son—more powerful and impressive.

How about describing their god with the words—omnipotent, infallible, immaterial, and omnipresent? These were the branding words that many of the other more ancient gods had borrowed.

Though these words are mere cosmetic dressing, a large majority of followers still fall prey to the various religions, especially when hell and heaven had become the proverbial carrot dangled before them.

Have you ever wondered why past and existing major religious practices adopted anthropomorphism? Perhaps, a construct of theology around a god without human traits would be extremely difficult, if not impossible, to sell and propagate.

The results—if any—will be uninteresting. Let us not quickly forget that these gods or their trinity all have astral origins.

Remember the attributes of Horus? Those attributes always seem to permeate other gods around the world. The fact is: There are numerous "saviors" from around the world who subscribe to the numerous same attributes. These gods dominated different periods in time.

You may have noticed the birthdays of the gods. They were all born on December 25th. Though people are born on December 25, the birth of these gods was simply allegorically astrological.

Let us then summarize the similarities of a few solar gods for easy contrast.

| Characteristics | Sun | Jesus | Horus | Mithra | Attis | Krishna |
|---|---|---|---|---|---|---|
| As the Light | The light | The Light | The Light | The Light | The Light | The Light of the Sun |
| As the Word | Sometimes described as the Word | The Word | The Word | The Word | The Word | |
| The divine Sun | Celestial | Divine | Divine | Divine | Divine | Divine |
| As the Lamb | As the Guide | The Lamb of God | The Lamb of God | The Lamb of God | The Lamb of God | The Cow |
| Salvation | Brings salvation | Brings salvation | Brings salvation | Brings salvation | Brings salvation | Yes |
| Virgin Birth | Created by Consciousness | Yes | Yes | Yes | Yes | Yes |
| Born Dec. 25th | Yes | Yes | Yes | Yes | Yes | ? |
| Died | Died at lowest point | Died | Died | Died | Died | Died |
| Went to the underworld for 3 days | Yes | Yes | Yes | Yes | Yes | Yes |
| Risen from death | Yes | Yes | Yes | Yes | Yes | Yes |
| The Way | Yes | Yes | Yes | Yes | Yes | Yes |
| The Truth | Yes | Yes | Yes | Yes | Yes | Yes |

## The Greatest Celestial Deception

| | | | | | | |
|---|---|---|---|---|---|---|
| The Life | Yes | Yes | Yes | Yes | Yes | Yes |
| The Good Shepherd | Yes | Yes | Yes | Yes | Yes | Divine Herdsman |
| The Son of God | Yes | Yes | Yes | Yes | Yes | Yes |
| Mother—all versions of Isis except the sun | Consciousness—the Creator | Mary | Isis | Anahita | Nana | Devaki |
| Father | Consciousness—the Creator | Holy Ghost | Osiris | | Father in the Son, Son in the Father | Vasudev |
| The Lion of Judah | | Yes | | | | |
| The Alpha and Omega | Yes | Yes | Yes | Yes | Yes | 2nd in the Trinity |
| The Giver of Life | Yes | Yes | Yes | Yes | Yes | |
| The Bright Morning Star | Yes | Yes | | | | |
| Sun as Satan & Jesus | Yes | Yes | Yes | Yes | Yes | Yes |
| As the Light of the World | Yes | Yes | Yes | Yes | Yes | Yes |
| | | | | | | |
| At age 12 | Moving along the 12 zodiacs | Prodigal and teaching at age 12 | Teaching at age 12 | | | |
| At age 30 | Completes a zodiac | Gets baptized | Gets baptized | | | |
| Visited by 3 kings/stars | The stars aligned | Yes | Yes | Yes | Yes | Yes |
| Crucified and went to hell | Most high & lowest points | Yes | Yes | Yes | Yes | Yes |

| Sun went dark on crucifixion day | At lowest point | Yes | Yes | Yes | Yes | Yes |

At this juncture, it might be helpful to explain some aspects of astrology/astronomy, so that we understand the solstices. This will help to connect ideas and commonsensical thinking to understand the subsequent chapters that explain the facts, lies, allegories, and the falsity in the propaganda of religions.

Let us do a page or two on the solstices.

# Chapter Six    Solstices

A solstice is an astronomical happening. It is part of the ordained intelligence of the planetary system. A solstice happens twice a year in June and in December. A solstice is one of the planetary instructions—software, if you like—that must occur without fail.

This is so because the sun reaches its highest and lowest excursion relative to the celestial equator on the celestial sphere. It all has to do with the sun.

Solstices and the equinoxes are responsible for the seasons of the year.

The seasons are spring, summer, fall, and the winter, and at the top of their control is the sun. Can you imagine how important the sun is to seasons, like oxygen is to your survival? That is how important and a powerful celestial body the sun is.

It was that important then and that powerful today in the scheme of things, even in religions.

It will not be an overstatement to say that our forefathers had always been in awe of the stars, especially the sun. Even with all we know today, it is a given that without the sun, Earth will be a different—perhaps an uninhabitable—planet.

The word "solstice" is from Latin—*sol*, meaning sun, and the word *sistere,* meaning to stand still. Let's divert a little. Have you ever read in the Bible where it was said that the sun stood still? Here were two places and the quotes below: Joshua 10:13 (NRSV)

*And the sun stood still, and the moon stopped, until the nation took vengeance on their enemies. Is this not written in the Book of Jashar? The sun stopped in midheaven and did not hurry to set for about a whole day.*

Apocrypha's Sirach 46:4:

*Was it not through him that the sun stood still and one day became as long as two?*

So, when a solstice takes place, the sun stands still, so it seems, or, so the ancients described the phenomena.

Perhaps if you are one of those who read the Bible a lot, you may have read the parts above and wondered how that could be. Perhaps you were wondering if the books or the writers were wrong. The writers described what they witnessed in the best available words they had.

Solstice was what that description was referencing.

If someone observed this phenomenon from the North Pole, the sun ascends to the highest point in the sky just once a year in June—called the June solstice day.

If the observer was standing at the South Pole, the sun reaches the highest on the December solstice day. It follows that when there is summer solstice on one pole, there would be a winter solstice on the other pole.

Today, we understand with a great degree of certainty the continuous rotation of our planet. However, the sun's declination comes to a standstill at that moment of a solstice. You can, therefore, now, understand the sense in which solstice means "sun-standing."

For the purposes of the nitty-gritty of this book, it is important to understand the workings of the following stars—sun, Sirius, and the constellation Virgo, and, of course, the three kings/three sisters in Orion's Belt. Though not as an astrologer, enough research has been made to enable an explanation of the mentioned constellations.

These three bright stars—Alnitak, Alnilam, and Mintaka—are believed to have formed from the same nebula in Orion constellation.

# Chapter Seven    The Guide to the Sons of the Sun

How did the solar saviors become a thing? Was it because of ignorance? Was it just because of greed? Elites of the society seized on the ignorance of the masses because of greed to disinform and miseducate. Miseducation and rampant misinformation are still going on today, and of all places, in our institutions of higher learning!

The births were no mysteries, even though they were made to look so; neither were the deaths and resurrections. There was nothing religious in the concepts, even though it was made religious. There was nothing divine about the celestial bodies when such branding was used.

Indeed, there were no births, no deaths, and no resurrections. Reincarnations, maybe. It was all man's creations from misunderstood phenomena by our greedy, power-drunk forefathers.

## The Greatest Celestial Deception

What really boggles the mind today is that highly educated people were swallowed up by the allegorical juxtaposition of the misunderstood workings of the planetary system.

You remember the star, Sirius? Sirius is the brightest star in the night sky. It is also a binary star in Canis Major. It is referred to as the star in the East. On every December 24, it aligns with the three stars we sometimes refer to as the three kings/three sisters on Orion's Belt. They align and point to the place where the sunrise would take place on December 25th.

Ever heard of the three stars (three wise men or kings), follow the star in the east (Sirius) to locate the sunrise— the birth of the sun?

This is the alignment of the three stars located at Orion's Belt with Sirius to locate the sun that was undergoing solstice.

In the summer, the days are longer. Thus, from summer solstice to winter solstice, the daylight becomes shorter. It becomes colder too.

From an observer standing in the Northern Hemisphere, the sun appears to move south where it becomes even smaller, and the sunshine appears to get scarcer as we move through the winter.

The shortening of daylight and sunlight, and the accompanying harsh, cold weather leads to the suffocation and expiration of crops and greenery. This

# The Greatest Celestial Deception

crippling effect on plants and crops when approaching the winter solstice symbolized death to the ancient people. And all the death was linked to the effects of a dying sun.

By December 22nd, the sun's demise has fully taken place. What was happening to the sun is simply winter solstice. The sun had continually moved south for the past 6 months, and at this point, the sun has made it to the lowest point in the sky.

At this point, the sun is no longer moving south. Perceivably, the sun is standing still for 3 days. For 3 days, the sun resides near the Southern Crux (Cross).

Southern Cross is a constellation in the Southern Hemisphere of the sky. This constellation is only visible from latitudes south of 27 degrees. The 3 days the sun resides in Southern Cross are December 22nd, 23rd, and 24th.

Then on December 25th—Christmas Day—the sun moves 1 degree north. The sun reverts its journey. It is the beginning of the return to longer days. This is a beginning to spring and warmth and crop abundance.

Thus, it is said the sun died on the Cross (Constellation Crux), was dead for 3 days, and after the 3 days, the sun resurrected.

Right here was a simple concept. And as a concept, it was copied by many.

Therefore, Mithras, Horus, and numerous other solar saviors (sun gods) share the virgin birth mystery, the crucifixion, the 3 days death mystery, and finally, the resurrection.

So, how is the sun a savior? I am betting on your understanding of agriculture and perhaps biology to answer this. Just imagine if the sun does not return. That will signal the extinction of plants, and no food means no animals.

It is the sun's transition movements to and from the Northern Hemisphere that brings seasons, especially spring, which brings about the growth of plants and therefore salvation.

Something is missing. Where do the mothers of the solar saviors fit in all the stories of these gods? For all the solar saviors there was a mother who had a virgin birth. Virgo became Isis. Virgo also became the virgin mother. The most important take here is that this is all about a constellation Virgo. Virgo is the second-largest constellation in the sky.

Perhaps, there is a need to explain to differentiate a constellation and a zodiac. Constellations are a group of stars. They form patterns and are named and identified by their traditional mythological figures.

Zodiacs are also constellations, but all constellations are not zodiac constellations. This is because zodiac constellations are those specific 12 which are passed by the sun yearly.

Simply put, zodiac constellations are the Taurus, Leo, Pisces, Aries, etcetera.

Virgo has thus far metamorphosed into many names, but one of the characteristics she retains is virginity. Today, the most popular of all the named virgins is Mary. It was and still is the constellation Virgo.

There is a city called Bethlehem on earth. Bethlehem, when translated from Hebrew, reads: House of Bread. The constellation Virgo is also referred to as the House of Bread.

In fact, if you look closely at a depiction of Virgo, you will see the "virgin mother" holding in her right hand a branch and in her left hand, some sheaves of corn or seeds of wheat.

There are different interpretations for the crop symbols, but one is most interesting.

A House of Bread—a symbolic representation with wheat—represents August and September, the period of crop harvest.

Some have, however, interpreted the same symbol as a reference or representation of seed of the woman—the virgin—who will conceive and bear a child.

They seek to put as evidence to support this interpretation as truth by quoting Isaiah 7:14 (KJV):

## The Greatest Celestial Deception

*Therefore, the Lord himself will give you a sign: Behold, the virgin shall conceive and bear a Son, and shall call his name Immanuel.*

Now that we know the literal meaning and reference to the constellation Virgo as House of Bread, meaning Bethlehem, it is a place in the cosmos, not a place and city on this planet.

If you have not already come to an understanding that the whole documentation of the sun's ecliptic travels across the zodiacs was the basis for the play-by-play narration story of the solar saviors, perhaps a little explaining of the 12 zodiacs/12 disciples of the sun would do it.

# Chapter Eight Why Easter Is Celebrated in the Spring

Again, it was/is all astrological.

Easter is a festival that celebrates the resurrection of Jesus from the dead. Some say it is a celebration of the rebirth of Jesus Christ.

Is it really? Wink. Wink.

Remember December 22nd, 23rd, and 24th, the days the sun was "dead" and "rose" on December 25th?

Do you ever wonder why the resurrection was/is not celebrated on December 25th? Was that not the birth or rebirth?

The day the sun reappeared after 3 days in Sheol in the depths of hell—a place the holy books referred to as the deepest bottom of the pit.

The celebration of the rebirth or resurrection could not happen immediately following the rebirth, not until the spring equinox—the moment the plane of Earth's equator passes through the center of the sun's disk.

The Greatest Celestial Deception

This happens around March 20, depending on the type of calendar. Thus, the March equinox, also called the northward equinox, is the equinox we see on Earth as the subsolar point appears to leave the Southern Hemisphere and cross the celestial equator onward to the Northern Hemisphere.

As this point, the sun has overpowered death, the long darkness—the evil one—as the daylight becomes longer and plant life begins to sprout, and the revitalization process across the land is fully started and noticeable.

At the spring, daylight is approximately 12 hours long and increasing as the season progresses.

# Chapter Nine   Cross of the Zodiac, Cross of the Disciples

As you read and react to this chapter, bear in mind that this is about astrology and astronomy and not a whole bunch related to the reasonableness of a Jesus Christ—The Son of a God.

The sun is real. You and I can see it. Even without science, yes, we can feel, ionize it, get chlorophyll by it, live by it, and even play outside in its rays (spirit) daily—at least on most days as we dive in and out of the rivers and oceans of the world.

Sometimes, we run from it to avoid its intense rays. There is no denying the effects of the sun. The sun can always be confirmed.

The sun, you can see, and you can confirm. You can fool most of the people sometimes, but you cannot fool all the people all the time. This was a line in a song by a very popular singer—Bob Marley. Bob Marley seemed to be echoing the lines at the beginning of this book about the deception inflicted on the people of this planet by those whose intent it was/is to grab all that needed to be grabbed.

Can you now appreciate some of the art of deception? If not, let us learn astronomy and see how those who understood it used it for grand-style deception.

In astrology and astronomy, the zodiac is a circle of twelve 30-degree divisions of the celestial longitude that are centered on the ecliptic longitude—a path for the sun's movements along the celestial arena over the course of the year.

The zodiacs and the periods the sun spun past them are listed below:

1. Aquarius (Jan. 20–Feb. 18)—The Water Bearer is the 11th astrological sign in the zodiac, originating from the constellation Aquarius. Aquarius is situated between Capricornus and Pisces.
2. Pisces (Feb. 19–Mar. 20)—The Fish. Pisces is a constellation of the zodiac. It is between Aquarius to the west and Aries to the east. The ecliptic and the celestial equator intersect within Pisces and in Virgo.
3. Aries (Mar. 21–April 19)—The Ram. Aries is the first astrological sign in the zodiac. Aries

# The Greatest Celestial Deception

   occupies the first 30 degrees of celestial longitude.
4. Taurus (April 20–May 20)—The Bull. The sun going into Taurus coincides with spring, a season when all of nature is in full revitalization. Taurus is another constellation of the zodiac. It is a prominent constellation in the Northern Hemisphere. The sun passes through this constellation between April 20th–May 20th.
5. Gemini (May 21–June 20)—The Twins. Gemini is another one of those constellations in the zodiac. The Twins signify double or abundance of produce (crops). The sun resides in this zodiac between May 21st and June 20th. This constellation has 85 stars when observed from planet Earth with the naked eyes.
6. Cancer (June 21–July 22)—The Crab. Cancer is one of the members of the zodiac. The sun travels through Cancer from June 21st and July 22nd.
7. Leo (July 23–Aug. 22)—The Lion. Leo is a member of the twelve 30-degree divisions of the longitude. This constellation of the zodiac lies between Cancer to the west and Virgo to the east. The sun roars at its fiercest when in this zodiac.
8. Virgo (Aug. 23–Sep. 22)—The Virgin. Virgo is the 6th astrological sign of the zodiac. Virgo is looked at as the Virgin. Virgo is said to be the second-largest constellation. The symbol of Virgo—sheaves of wheat or seeds of corn, means quite a few things to different divides of peoples.

9. Libra (Sep. 23–Oct. 22)—The Scales. Libra is the 7th astrological sign of the zodiac. The sun transits this celestial longitude between September 23rd and October 22nd. Under the sidereal zodiac, the sun transits this constellation from approximately October 16 to November 17. The Scales symbolism is from the Scales of Justice held by Themis—the Greek goddess of divine law and order.
10. Scorpio (Oct. 23–Nov. 21)—The Scorpion.
11. Sagittarius (Nov. 22–Dec. 21)—The Archer. Also, one of the constellations of the zodiacs, Sagittarius—the Archer—moves toward the southern sky of summer. Sagittarius is mythical as he is half man, half horse with his bow drawn and pointed at Antares, the bright red heart of Scorpius—the scorpion. It was said that the Archer was avenging Orion who was slain by the sting of a scorpion.
12. Capricorn (Dec. 22–Jan. 19)—The Horned Goat.

The following chapter will center on how the zodiacs and mostly the sun were individualized. The sun was essentially the boss, who, at any given month, can change positions. And depending on that position, the sun moves to a "Most High" position in the sky—the heavens or becomes Lucifer at the bottom of the pit—hell or Sheol.

In other words, the sun can be Jesus Christ at one instant and Lucifer at another instant. The sun can be at one point today and be at another point tomorrow. By the Bible's acknowledgment, all the above is true. By astronomy, they were true and are still true today.

But all the allegories assigned to the sun are not at all true. Not even one is true because when you start off with a false premise, all you elucidate are lies.

No one is making this up, but it doubly exposes the ignorance some few people tried to exploit in ancient times. Our beliefs today were the extension of the ancient practices, no matter the angle from which you looked at it.

The sun was/is just one of the many celestial bodies anthropomorphized. The moon too was made a god in various places around the world. Sin was the Sumerian moon god. Sumerians occupied Mesopotamia more than 3,000 years ago—the territories of today's Iraq and Kuwait. With a lineage of An(u), Sin was the child of Enlil and Ninlil. Sin was worshipped in the city of Ur. The moon god has many names signifying different phases of the moon, like Nanna being the full moon, Sin the crescent moon, and Asimbabbar—the beginning of each lunar cycle.

There are others too many to list in this narrative. Though we live in a world of posttruth environment, truth cannot be hidden. Sometimes, the truth is like

# The Greatest Celestial Deception

an iceberg, two-thirds of it hidden under water, but it will always be out there for us to discover. The truth is like a foul fart in an enclosed space. The stink will always spread, no matter your desire that others not smell the stink. If you poop under the river, the poop will surface. It is like the truth.

If a thief stole a banana and dove into the river with intent to conceal the loot, he might succeed for a while. It is said that a banana peel peeled under the water will float up to the surface. No truth can go hidden forever, even if you try to conceal it.

No one is begotten to ignorance. By now, you may have already reached the level in this book where you have started questioning your personal beliefs. Think about it for only a minute.

# Chapter Ten
# Individualizing the Sun and the Stars & Destroying Fake Legacies

Today, you can read various historical writings of events and practices where solar gods refer to themselves as, among others—the light, the light of the world, the lion, and the star. We are told in the book of Revelation that Jesus called himself "the bright morning star."

What is "the morning star"?

In ancient times, and even in early astronomy, the morning star was the brightest star in the sky. It is the light of the world. Do you really want an answer to the question "what is the bright morning star"?

Perhaps we should find a reason why Jesus referred to himself as the "bright morning star." Again, knowing what you know now, did you ever fathom that the "bright morning star" can speak?

Of course not! And this answer is reasonable.

What the practices were at that time and what the writers did then was the personification of celestial bodies—the stars. The solar gods were the personification of celestial bodies as deities. Even the use of religious books of record for evidence would point to the same historical writings and depictions from ancient whispers.

From the book of Isaiah 14:12–16, we read about the personification of the sun. You may wish to read the whole chapter. Let's read from the NIV:

*$^{12}$ How you have fallen from heaven, morning star, son of the dawn! You have been cast down to the earth, you who once laid low the nations!*
*$^{13}$ You said in your heart, "I will ascend to the heavens; I will raise my throne above the stars of God; I will sit enthroned on the mount of assembly, on the utmost heights of Mount Zaphon.*
*$^{14}$ I will ascend above the tops of the clouds; I will make myself like the Most High."*

*¹⁵ But you are brought down to the realm of the dead, to the depths of the pit.*
*¹⁶ Those who see you stare at you, they ponder your fate: "Is this the man who shook the earth and made kingdoms tremble . . ."*

Here, you must have known immediately that the sun was being discussed. The movement of the sun from its celestial highest point to the lowest point was a marvel to the ancients. They were wowed! They did not understand it. So, sometimes they worried that the sun might not appear, and when it does, it becomes such a mystery that it must be deified.

Now, I have asked some people well versed in their religious books the meaning of the above. The above verses were immediately equated with Lucifer—Satan—and the decreed punishment.

In fact, the King James Version literally translates "Morning Star" as Lucifer. Here it is:

*¹² How art thou fallen from heaven, O Lucifer, son of the morning! How art thou cut down to the ground, which didst weaken the nations!*
*¹³ For thou hast said in thine heart, I will ascend into heaven, I will exalt my throne above the stars of God: I will sit also upon the mount of the congregation, in the sides of the north:*

*¹⁴ I will ascend above the heights of the clouds; I will be like the Most High.*

*15 Yet thou shalt be brought down to hell, to the sides of the pit.*

*16 They that see thee shall narrowly look upon thee, and consider thee, saying, is this the man that made the earth to tremble . . .*

What you must glean from the above are:

1. From verse 12—"fallen from heaven" means descent of the sun.
2. From verse 13—"in the sides of the north"—Northern Hemisphere.
3. From verse 14—"Most High" literally means most high point.
4. From verse 15—"brought down to hell/Sheol/pit" is the lowest point that occurs on December 22nd, 23rd, and 24th.

Just a simple reminder: Do you recall the story we are continuously told of how Satan fell out of favor with God? Of how Satan was cast down to earth with his fallen angels? The above verses from Isaiah seem to corroborate and justify that story.

However, this does not eliminate or negate in any way whatsoever my opinions in my other books of the existence of aliens that lived on earth for eons of years before they decided to create humans.

# The Greatest Celestial Deception

The physical sciences have established the logic of observable facts. The physical sciences have carried apparatuses into the depths of space and have debunked some of the assumptions and understandings of the ancient peoples. Our planet has been proven not to be the center of the universe, after all; instead, the earth is one of the smallest bodies that revolve around our sun, which is the center of our planetary system.

Every bright star that shines in space is now ascertained to be another sun, and like Earth's sun, they are also the center of a system of dependent planets. From science, we now know that there is an innumerable number of these planetary systems moving "intelligently" throughout the boundless expanse of space. These systems are usually found to be separated by very long distances—distances that will continue to extend.

While looking at the expanse of space with human eyes and telescopes, it is difficult to fathom the distance between the bodies, planets, and the planetary systems from one another as the bodies and systems look clustered. The distances are just incommensurable for our minds to process.

Think about this for a few seconds, and then juxtapose our Earth onto the universe. If this does not blow your mind, I wonder what will. It should make you wonder about our importance in the scheme of things in the universe.

Perhaps you should also juxtapose religion onto Earth and wonder whether an Earth that is almost an imperceptible dot needs a Jesus to save it. And that you are part of this Earth, and this universe is reason enough to think and marvel but not on religious lines. Who cares what you think anyway? So, think in whatever fashion you so desire.

Think along the lines of why you found yourself on Earth, and your life adapted to it. Since all things created or evolved was because of some purpose, have you considered that other planets have life specifically adapted for those planets? Or did you think that all life must look human?

Science has, of course, proven that there is the existence of planets everywhere, and since there is a purpose for everything evolved, there is life in these planets just as life is as infinite as the universes (multiverse) . . . Life of beings able to survive those environments, visible or invisible.

Often, people's efforts to have other people reflect the Bible's point of view in a narrative is a frequent point of tension. We have and will continue to have the same dissensions when dedicated scholars inject meanings/interpretations borrowing from our modern understanding of the universe.

Now that you have read and understood it for yourself, can you connect any dots that make that ancient story logical and reasonable?

Still on the bright morning star, while the above Isaiah chapter debases the morning star as Lucifer, the book of Revelation extols the morning star as Jesus. Revelation 22:16 (NIV) states:

*I, Jesus, have sent my angel to give you this testimony for the churches. I am the Root and the Offspring of David, and the bright Morning Star.*

There is a problem in that verse, especially the "I am the Root and the Offspring of David" part. If the religion is claiming a miraculous virgin birth, it means Jesus had no human father and thus, no lineage to King David. Judaism teaches that the Messiah will be born like a regular human being. Jesus was not regularly born. This apart, did you notice the bright Morning Star part?

Why are both Jesus and Satan described as the "Morning Star"? While you are pondering the question, you will be surprised that there are other recurring themes. This is because the solar gods' themes are borrowed from one source.

For example, Jesus was not exclusively referred to as Lion of Judah in Revelation 5:5 (NIV).

*Then one of the elders said to me, "Do not weep! See, the Lion of the tribe of Judah, the Root of David, has triumphed. He is able to open the scroll and its seven seals."*

Satan was also referred to as a lion in 1 Peter 5:8 (NIV):

## The Greatest Celestial Deception

*Be alert and of sober mind. Your enemy the devil prowls around like a roaring lion looking for someone to devour.*

The explanation provided was that Jesus as lion is king, royal, and majestic, and Satan as lion is the bad one looking for whom to devour. These explanations were simply conjured up and were illogical yesterday like they are unreasonable today, as you have seen so far.

So, what else has been personified from the celestial longitudes? The zodiacs have been personified to be the disciples of the sun. The sun is the brightest of all the stars and moves along the constellations bringing light to all the places it passes.

There are many characteristics used to describe the gods. At least two of those characteristics were omnipresence and omnipotence. Let's consider the one most used characteristic further.

# Chapter Eleven
# Omnipresence of Solar Gods

Omnipresence or ubiquity is the doctrine of being present everywhere. This concept is usually associated with religious practices in veneration of deities or a supreme being. Accordingly, believers justify this characteristic for the deities by rehearsing some verses in their texts.

So, to say that any god is omnipresent is saying that that god is present everywhere. Some religions take this property even further to include transcendence and immanence of that god.

That god is everywhere always means that his all-seeing eyes are a witness to all that you always do.

In other words, if you stole, raped, or killed, among other bad things, and while no one saw you do those bad things, rest assured that God saw you.

People are taught these things, and there is the insistence by your religion that you believe and accept that it is the truth by faith.

Put aside what you have been told all these years and, once again, let us read from Psalm 139:7–10 (NRSV):

*7 Where can I go from your spirit? Or where can I flee from your presence?*

*8 If I ascend to heaven, you are there; if I make my bed in Sheol, you are there.*

*9 If I take the wings of the morning and settle at the farthest limits of the sea,*

*10 Even there your hand shall lead me, and your right hand shall hold me fast.*

In the above verses, there are three key words/suggestions to decipher the meaning quickly. There is heaven, Sheol, and the suggestion of movement/presence.

You may have your own inference already but put that aside too and use the keywords so that we do not fall into the disinformation trap.

It was a reference once again to the movement of the sun. A movement of the sun to its highest and lowest points—the heavens and Sheol (hell). Verse 7's "Where can I go from your spirit? Or where can I flee from your presence?" is a refrain for: The sun is everywhere. The sun is the light of this world and some other planets.

By now, the world has learned much more about the universe. We know that there are many stars with planets in orbit. The Milky Way might have as many as 400 billion suns according to scientific estimates.

# Chapter Twelve  The Ages & the End of the World

The center of most religions is a promise of eternal enjoyment or eternal punishment. The word *rapture*—a sudden transport of a believer from Earth to heaven at the Second Coming of Christ—is part of a teaching in some religious circles.

The rapture is supposed to usher in a new world for those raptured. By a new world, one is not sure if this means just Earth or the whole universe.

The primary scripture passage on the rapture is found on 1 Thessalonians 4:13–18. Let us read from NRSV:

*13 But we do not want you to be uninformed, brothers and sisters, about those who have died, so that you may not grieve as others do who have no hope.*

*14 For since we believe that Jesus died and rose again, even so, through Jesus, God will bring with him those who have died. 15 For this we declare to you by the word of the Lord, that we who are alive, who are left until the coming of the Lord, will by no means precede those who have died.*

*16 For the Lord himself, with a cry of command, with the archangel's call and with the sound of God's trumpet, will descend from heaven, and the dead in Christ will rise first. ¹⁷ Then we who are alive, who are left, will be caught up in the clouds together with them to meet the Lord in the air; and so, we will be with the Lord forever.*

*¹⁸ Therefore encourage one another with these words.*

When the above rapture will take place is mostly speculation. Some are pointing to the Age of Aquarius as the end of times.

As you may have observed, the stories in the Bible employ anthropomorphism to allegorize the characters in the stories. The stories are a reiteration of astrology, and the stories spanned over 3 ages while predicting the next—Aquarius.

Luke 22:10 (NRSV) described Aquarius.

*"Listen," he said to them, "when you have entered the city, a man carrying a jar of water will meet you; follow him into the house he enters."*

Notwithstanding the context of the verse above, the injection of this verse says a lot when understood. The man carrying a jar of water is the symbol of the Age of Aquarius. The Age of Aquarius is the house or a given period.

Before we delve fully into the various ages, it would be nice to read Matthew 28:20 (NRSV).

*and teaching them to obey everything that I have commanded you. And remember, I am with you always, to the end of the age.*

You know that the sun will always be with the living to the end of the age, Aquarius, and much thereafter.

End of age does not translate to end of times like some would have you believe. Indeed, the same verse taken from King James Version (KJV) may be misleading, in that age translated into an end to our world. Here it is:

*Teaching them to observe all things whatsoever I have commanded you: and, lo, I am with you always, even unto the end of the world. Amen.*

Therefore, a discussion about how the ages work is important here. An astrological age is a period in astrologic theology where astrologers insinuate parallels some important shifts in the developmental progression of humankind.

These changes can occur in areas of cultures, new societies, and new politics. It could be a period where humans don't walk long distances anymore as a way of travel but use motorized travel and air travel to and from various earthly and even planetary positions.

The Greatest Celestial Deception

There are 12 astrological ages, though all the Bible stories took center stage within three ages while predicting a new one—Aquarius.

One astrological age is 72 years multiplied by 30 degrees of a given zodiac = 2,160 years.

The one cycle of 12 ages would, therefore, be approximately 26,000 years.

There is this phenomenon—the procession of the equinoxes—that completes its process in 2,160 years—an age. The ancients referred to the approximate 2,160 years as an age.

By the way, when we calculate the sum of all the ages, it is referred to as the "great year"; perhaps, like me, you also did a multiplication of 2,160 years by 12 = 25,920 years.

Meanwhile, it is said that from BC 4300 to BC 2150, that was the age of Taurus—the Bull.

BC 2150 to AD 1 was the year of Aries—the Ram. The next age is even more of a paradigm shift. It is the Age of Pisces. AD 1 to AD 2150—the Age of Pisces—the age we are still in and represented by the symbol of a fish.

The Age of Pisces is very spectacular. It is not spectacular because of anything other than that there was a pronounced change, perhaps a paradigm shift of a change. Perhaps you will describe this change as one where suddenly man's intelligence took a monstrous leap. It was/is an age in which mankind's abilities in all spheres of endeavors exploded.

Truthfully, it is so.

We suddenly became smart, so much so, we are even questioning the "gods." It was quite a leap from banana-munching Homo sapiens who lived in the caves to intelligently thinking humanoids.

The next age—AD 2150 to AD 4300—predicted in the Bible or perhaps by "Jesus" is Aquarius. Saying it was "predicted" is perhaps being respectfully polite because, in the matter of logic and reason, there was no prediction there.

As an aside, this is the age that so many uninformed religionists, particularly Christians, presume to be the end of the world.

The scientifically proven truth for the ages is that it works as a cycle. Be it drummed loud and clear that at the end of a cycle, a new cycle begins. The celestial bodies are more precise than our human clocks.

There are various methods to calculate the length of an astrological age. Therefore, there are variations in the length of an astrological age as there is variation in the total number of years. Today, some astrologers think we are still in the Age of Pisces, while others say we have entered the House of Aquarius already.

Ages are based on constellations in the heavens rather than on seasons on which we base our calculations here on Earth. Some constellations are bigger than others; therefore, what decides when one age ends and another begins is an approximation.

Accordingly, different astrologers approximated calculation for when we enter the Age of Aquarius. They range from AD 1447, suggested by Terry MacKinnell, to AD 3597, given by John Addey.

Before Aries was the Age of Taurus—the Bull. Moses entered the House of Aries. Perhaps you remember the story from Exodus. Moses went away for quite some time, and the Israelites saw that Moses delayed coming down from the mountain. They decided they would go back and make for themselves a god. Let the Bible, Exodus 32:1–4 (NRSV), tell the story:

*When the people saw that Moses delayed to come down from the mountain, the people gathered around Aaron, and said to him, "Come, make gods for us, who shall go before us; as for this Moses, the man who brought us up out of the land of Egypt, we do not know what has become of him." [2] Aaron said to them, "Take off the gold rings that are on the ears of your wives, your sons, and your daughters, and bring them to me." ³ So all the people took off the gold rings from their ears, and brought them to Aaron. ⁴ He took the gold from them, formed it in a mold, and cast an image of a calf; and they said, "These are your gods, O Israel, who brought you up out of the land of Egypt!"*

You can see right away that the people chose a bull. The significance of this was that the people chose the House of the Bull—an age—and a zodiac sign they knew. They anthropomorphized what to them was God. It was no different from what has been done with the solar gods.

# Chapter Thirteen   They Made Fools of Us

The word for character in ancient Greek was *ethos* from which was derived the word "ethics." Heraklitos opined that a person's ethos is their *daimon*, meaning "fate." It then follows that a man's character is his fate. The ancient Greeks held that character is fate.

I know a chef who would rather talk about character in a different manner. The chef has this persistent quip every time I met him at his restaurant. He would be heard saying, "You are what you eat." I understood this to mean: Your body is a representation of your eating habits. The comments above, though, are about character, but it applies to your mind too. Be careful what you feed your mind because the mind is everything you feed it.

I cannot describe who or what God is, but I know what God is not. I know what a sun and a moon are. They are celestial bodies. They fed the stars to our ancients' minds as the gods. They also fed such celestial bodies to our fathers' minds, so much so, our fathers look like fools now.

Our fathers were not idiots but wise men who were conned with trickery and deceit while their minds were crippled with disinformation. The greedy leaders/smarter ones among them were those who established what there was and what there is to be as a means to an end.

The smarter ones were the vessels of these modern religions which are a regurgitation of old practices.

Our forefathers' practices were no different from what we, their progenitors, are doing today or next Friday or Sunday. It will be no different for subsequent Fridays and Sundays; and next Easters and Christmases.

Neither you nor I could have fathomed that old cultural practices of the ancient era would ever have been koshered into our new religions were it not for researchers. And we pretend like ours are better than theirs as we deem their practices as paganism. We are terribly and ignorantly very arrogant.

I hope someday we will wake up to see the foolishness of our religions. Would that be too much to ask?

What do you feel like doing now that you know that you'd been had, religious-wise? Angry—huh? Angry at the cover-ups or angry at an author who has studied nights and days for years to expose a truth for you?

Some authors live in parts of the world where freedom of expression flourishes. I feel for those who must succumb to regional or sectional interpretations of a belief, for if you are a reader or writer, your abilities to express yourself may have been taken away.

It may be taken away not because what you are about to say is foolishness, but because it is so wise, the authorities may not be able to control the people as they do now.

Beliefs where dissent is not allowed and complaints disavowed are what most people refer to as religions. Think of a religion. Any religion. Think what that religion teaches. At the end of your thought process, you must have figured that that religion imposes restrictions, tells you what to do, even what to eat and how to behave. Religion becomes for you a driving and a dividing force, a disease masquerading as a cure, and a disguise for racism. Religion disables reality checks. It encourages believers to believe in anthropomorphic beings of untestable existence. As such, religion becomes an enabler for you. Religion enables stupidity, but you hardly would notice that. Religions, when you understand it, are an insult and debasing of the one true Consciousness.

But what exactly is religion? Religion is simply an instrument for control. Religion is a carryover of the misunderstanding of the concept of yin and yang—Oneness. But that concept was not fully understood.

You remember Seth and Horus? The commanders of the day and the night? That suddenly transformed into the light and darkness conundrum? The good and the bad divide? The God and the Satan question? That finally metamorphosed into a savior or the destroyer—Satan.

The Greatest Celestial Deception

Please understand that every living or dead thing is the rendition of our universe.

# Chapter Fourteen
# Historical or Historicized Jesus

Almost everything we know about the historical Jesus comes from the four New Testament Gospels of Matthew, Mark, Luke, and John.

The Gospels are believed by non-Christian scholars to be written several decades after Jesus supposedly died. I thought that your mind might have been made at this point. But if you are still confused and doubtful, feel free to reminisce somehow that Jesus walked the earth and consider the additional presentations of materials.

When you read about the pharaohs, Horus, or the pyramids scattered—all over the world—you also read about the evidence discovered as they dig up the ground and the findings displayed for anyone interested to see.

More items are still being unearthed and discovered to this very day. The museums housing the unearthed materials are the confirmation that there was a historical existence of the subjects depicted on those artifacts.

There are physical bodies of pharaohs or pharaonic priests unearthed now and then. The Sphinx is standing there to be seen by all the gawking eyes from around the world.

But nothing, not even a clearly dated material writing, has been attested to and associated with Jesus Christ. There has been no archaeological or other physical evidence for Jesus' existence as a man who walked the earth.

However, most Christian scholars agree that Jesus did exist. They claim Jesus was born sometime in a decade before the Common Era. They also estimate that he died during the years the Roman governor Pontius Pilate ruled Judea around 26–36 CE. If there isn't any archaeological evidence, it is because they will not find any. But, if you look in the right places, Jesus is the bright morning star, and you can't miss it.

So, naturally, the questions follow. Did Jesus really exist or was he just concocted? What is, if any, the historical evidence that Jesus lived? If you have read this far, I am almost certain you have an answer.

Perhaps, you feel an urge to ask if there was a need to reask these questions after the mounting evidence provided reading from their book.

The answer was in the book. All you need to do is read it, and voilà, there was the answer all along.

Jesus' believers say that the idea that the Bible cannot be considered a source that could be relied on is absurd.

Believers believe that the Bible is a very good source for reliable evidence about Jesus' historical existence.

Obviously, I am tempted to ask if the person I will be engaging knows fully well how the Bible was put together.

These are the same religionists who believe by faith.

Over the past few years, I have become well-aware of the harm that religions and other dogmas have had on every continent, that the evidence and logic for either agnosticism or atheism seemed glaringly obvious and advantageously better for any well-educated person.

Ordinarily, some of us would be elated when religion becomes less important in the day-to-day lives of the living. Some have expressed fear if that happened. Whatever their fears, it resulted from those teachings they imbibed in from their religion. Their need to be faithful has a stronger pull than the evidence presented.

So, when I come across arguments drawing evidence from faith, we should do more to counter the poison that religions had injected into the veins of the faithful. We don't just have to fold our hands akimbo and give up.

And it won't be reasonable to allow such faithfully argued positions to seal such evidence. That some positions taken during debates might be faith-based would not disqualify the Bible and other "holy" books as a reliable source of information either.

If the intent was to deceive, the Bible would not be written in a manner that it ruins its own argument. And, boy, did the Bible ruin its own argument. Yes. A lot!

There is confidence in this assertion simply based on the criterion of embarrassment. The criterion of multiple attestation does not help either. Since there were multiple instances of the use of anthropomorphism and allegories, do you wonder why the criterion of multiple attestations is of no use?

If you remember our expanded discussion on the movement of the sun and the Earth, the equinoxes, the Ages, you will remember that the sun would be entering, or had entered, the House of Aquarius.

And even the Bible gave all the cues and clues.

Let's take instances we had used earlier from Luke 22:10 and Matthew 28:20.

Luke 22:10 (NRSV) described Aquarius.

*"Listen," he said to them, "when you have entered the city, a man carrying a jar of water will meet you; follow him into the house he enters."*

Remember that the man carrying a jar of water is the symbol of the Age of Aquarius. The Age of Aquarius is the "house" or a given period.

Again, in Matthew 28:20 (NRSV), the Age of Aquarius is repeated.

*and teaching them to obey everything that I have commanded you. And remember, I am with you always, to the end of the age.*

There are clear and convincing reasons to doubt Jesus' historical existence, especially after reading the preceding pages.

Some secular New Testament scholars have done some scholarly works on Jesus' historical existence. They mostly suggested in not very many words a historical Jesus.

As you read this work, perhaps you will understand why biblical scholar John Dominic Crossan described some of those works as "academic embarrassment."

Can you understand why? Can you put your finger on it?

If we must dig deeper, let us read some of Paul's Epistles, which some claim to be in existence earlier than the Gospels. I say, "they claimed," because if we doubt the historical existence of Jesus, Paul—a disciple—is not likely to exist.

By now, we know what the disciples were/are. But, when Paul's Epistles are examined, they too make no scholar to be dogmatic in the claim of Jesus' historical existence. The Epistles avoided discussing Jesus' activities on earth but delved into heavenly Jesus.

There is an interesting mention of various ages too. Now, when you connect heaven and ages, celestial bodies come to mind, and rightfully so. You may want to read a part of Paul's Epistle in Galatians 1:11–12 (NRSV):

> *For I want you to know, brothers and sisters, that the gospel that was proclaimed by me is not of human origin; [12] for I did not receive it from a human source, nor was I taught it, but I received it through a revelation of Jesus Christ.*

This is a dead giveaway that Jesus Christ was not human but *humanized* and *historicized*. By the above, Paul ruled out human sources for his teaching.

In another instance, the Pauline Epistles instead suggested, so overwhelmingly, a solar Jesus in 1 Corinthians 2:6–10 (NRSV):

*[6] Yet among the mature we do speak wisdom, though it is not a wisdom of this age or of the rulers of this age, who are doomed to perish. [7] But we speak God's wisdom,*

*secret and hidden, which God decreed before the ages for our glory. ⁸ None of the rulers of this age understood this; for if they had, they would not have crucified the Lord of glory. ⁹ But, as it is written,*

*"What no eye has seen, nor ear heard,
nor the human heart conceived,
what God has prepared for those who love him"—*

*¹⁰ these things God has revealed to us through the Spirit; for the Spirit searches everything, even the depths of God.*

Does anything above strike you? In verse 6, "not a wisdom of this age or of the rulers of this age . . ." should strike you. All the above was a narration of celestial bodies—the rulers and deciders of ages. Most of it. All of it.

Even the use of the word *Spirit* in verse 10 refers to the reach of the sun. The sun is Sol. Sol as Sunna is the sun personified in many mythoi, including Germanic mythology. The above was not helping to establish a human Jesus one bit.

Some of the mainstream non-Christian scholars kept struggling to prove the existence of a historical Jesus, but they keep coming up short because there was no way to trace the human historical Jesus. It just did not exist unless you want to manufacture that historical existence.

It does not matter where you stand on this. If you understand what Jesus is, if Jesus walked this earth, your whole earth will be scorched into oblivion. We dogmatically know what Jesus is, and that Jesus was historicized.

If there was a human Jesus who walked this earth—you know already: Somebody assumed that name.

Do not bother. Hell doesn't exist. Satan, as Satan, was communicated to us and was a fabrication who does not exist as a being. If anything, you now know that when the sun is at its highest in the heavens, it becomes the "Most High in the heavens," and when the sun is at its lowest point in hell (the underworld), the sun became "Satan." The Book said so!

You read it here too. Heavens—meaning space—do exist, and you see it all the days of your life.

The sun too does exist, not that you need to be told that.

It won't be surprising now to hear those practicing Judaism say to you: "We told you Jesus was no Messiah." It will not surprise you; it would be understandable.

Perhaps you must have wondered why Judaism—an ancient monotheistic, Abrahamic religion with the Torah as its foundation book—doesn't recognize Jesus as the Messiah. You may suppose that if Jesus were of the lineage of King David, the Jews would know better. I retrieved part of an article I had once read. Here it is below with minimal changes for clarity.

> *Jewish eschatology is concerned with* moshiach *(the messiah) and* Olam Haba *(Hebrew for "the world to come"; i.e., the afterlife).*
>
> *The Hebrew word* moshiach *means the anointed one and refers to a mortal human being. While Christians use the word "messiah" as well, they use it in a different way. For many Christians, God's ultimate miracle was His Self-Incarnation as a human being. In this view, God was both fully man and yet also fully human, both limited in intelligence and yet omniscient, simultaneously.*
>
> *Philosophically and logically, these claims appear mutually incompatible. Yet the early church insisted that both truths be held together.*
>
> *How can God die? This thinking has always been foreign to Judaism. Within Judaism, moshiach is a human being who will be a descendant of King David, and who will usher in a messianic era of peace and prosperity for Israel and all the nations of the world. The job description, as such, is this:*

*1. All of the people of Israel will come back to Torah.*
*2. The people of Israel will be gathered back to the land of Israel.*
*3. The Holy Temple in Jerusalem will be rebuilt.*
*4. Israel will live among the nations as an equal and will be strong enough to defend herself.*
*5. Eventually, war, hatred, and famine will end, and an era of peace and prosperity will come upon the Earth.*

*The traditional Jewish understanding of the messiah is non-supernatural and is best elucidated by Maimonides (Rabbi Moshe ben Maimon), in his commentary to tractate Sanhedrin, of the Babylonian Talmud.*

*He writes:*

*"The Messianic age is when the Jews will regain their independence and all return to the land of Israel. The Messiah will be a very great king; he will achieve great fame, and his reputation among the gentile nations will be even greater than that of King Solomon. His great righteousness and the wonders that he will bring about will cause all peoples to make peace with him and all lands to serve him . . . Nothing will change in the Messianic age, however, except that Jews will regain their independence. Rich and poor, strong and weak, will still exist. However, it will be very easy for*

*people to make a living, and with very little effort they will be able to accomplish very much . . . it will be a time when the number of wise men will increase . . . war shall not exist, and nation shall no longer lift sword against nation . . . The Messianic age will be highlighted by a community of the righteous and dominated by goodness and wisdom. It will be ruled by the Messiah, a righteous and honest king, outstanding in wisdom, and close to God. Do not think that the ways of the world or the laws of nature will change; this is not true. The world will continue as it is. The prophet Isaiah predicted 'The wolf shall live with the sheep; the leopard shall lie down with the kid.' This, however, is merely allegory, meaning that the Jews will live safely, even with the formerly wicked nations. All nations will return to the true religion [monotheism, although not necessarily Judaism] and will no longer steal or oppress. Note that all prophecies regarding the Messiah are allegorical—Only in the Messianic age will we know the meaning of each allegory and what it comes to teach us. Our sages and prophets did not long for the Messianic age in order that they might rule the world and dominate the gentiles . . . the only thing they wanted was to be free for Jews to involve themselves with the Torah and its wisdom."*

If you want to read the article in its entirety, it is here: www.fact-index.com/j/je/jewish_eschatology.html. You see right away that historically, Jesus did not fulfill any of the messianic prophecies. The Messiah was supposed to be born to regular parents and be a regular human.

According to Jewish sources, the Messiah must be descended on his father's side from King David, but the Christian claim of a virgin birth makes Jesus fatherless (humanwise); therefore, Jesus could not possibly have fulfilled the messianic prophecy of being descended from his father's side of King David.

The attempt to link Joseph to the lineage of King David, even if true, does not cut it. If anything, it makes rubbish of the virgin birth.

The Christian take on Jesus is that of a mysterious birth and of the trinity signifying that Jesus was not a regular human. If you now know what Jesus is, you already know that Jesus was not human at all. And Jesus is alive, though not human nor Creator God.

Though Christians claim that Jesus will fulfill the prophecies in his Second Coming, Jewish sources counter, saying that the fulfillment of the messianic prophecies was supposed to occur outright in the First Coming because there was no concept of a "Second" Coming.

The truth of the matter is: There was no First Coming, and there won't be a Second Coming.

# Chapter Fifteen
# Conclusion—Behold the Light of the World

Man has been wearing blinders for ages, and now the blinders have come off. The perception of religions has been managed and directed for so long that communities simply cower to the teachings with no questions asked.

The perception is so well managed you fail to even think about the *mis*perceptions. And the misperceptions are many with dire consequences to living your life as was predetermined and prerecorded in the Akashic realm.

Though our religious histories have helped shape our thought processes and belief systems, rightly or wrongly, is it not time to remove the blinders?

I will use Christianity, which I was part of for many years, as the example to help exhibit some of the misperceptions.

If you know Jesus, you know that Jesus is the Light of the World . . .

If you know Jesus, you know that Jesus is majestic . . .

If you know Jesus, you know how Jesus saves the world . . .

If you know Jesus, you know how Jesus brings salvation . . .

If you know Jesus, you know how Jesus brings light . . .

If you know Jesus, you know that Jesus is with you daily . . .

If you understand, you know Jesus will rise again . . .

When you understand, you know Jesus will be with mankind till the end of the ages . . .

When you understand, you know how Jesus walked on water . . .

When you understand the ages, you can imagine how Jesus was born . . .

When you understand, you understand the death of Jesus . . .

And you know the 3 days in Sheol—in the deepest part of the pit of hell . . .

And you would have understood the exact time Jesus will come again majestically . . .


But, who or what is this Jesus? Does Jesus exist? Oh yes! Jesus exists but conclusively not as a human

> or Son of a God but as a sun—a star showing the majesty of the Creator—Consciousness. The sun is the handiwork of the Intelligent Creator.

The practices of Pharaoh King Akhenaten finally came home to the world to roost.

And you see Jesus almost every day.

We may not have expatiated on a very important piece of information given to us on a platter of gold in a psalm—the 19th Psalm. Some psalms are simply songs of veneration used by earlier civilizations of Assyria, Sumer, Egypt, and others before they were co-opted and grafted into the book of Psalms and thus, the Bible.

Psalm 19 is a display of the truth of the ancients as they understood it before it was grafted into the Bible.

Yet, we tend to read that page every time. If not, you are invited to read it below. You'd be surprised you will need no interpretation. Below is part of Psalm 19:1–6 from KJV and NRSV.

*The heavens declare the glory of God; and the firmament sheweth his handywork.*

*² Day unto day uttereth speech, and night unto night sheweth knowledge.*

*³ There is no speech nor language, where their voice is not heard.*

*⁴ Their line is gone out through all the earth, and their words to the end of the world. In them hath he set a tabernacle for the sun,*

*⁵ Which is as a bridegroom coming out of his chamber, and rejoiceth as a strong man to run a race.*

*⁶ His going forth is from the end of the heaven, and his circuit unto the ends of it: and there is nothing hid from the heat thereof.*

And the same verses from NRSV:

*¹ The heavens are telling the glory of God; and the firmament proclaims his handiwork.*
*² Day to day pours forth speech, and night to night declares knowledge.*
*³ There is no speech, nor are there words; their voice is not heard;*
*⁴ yet their voice goes out through all the earth, and their words to the end of the world. In the heavens he has set a tent for the sun,*
*⁵ which comes out like a bridegroom from his wedding*

*canopy,*
*and like a strong man runs its course with joy.*
*⁶ Its rising is from the end of the heavens, and its circuit to the end of them; and nothing is hid from its heat.*

As far back as 1793, Thomas Paine, 1737–1809, opined that:

> *The Book of Job and the 19th Psalm, which even the Church admits to be more ancient than the chronological order in which they stand in the book called the Bible, are theological orations conformable to the original system of theology. The internal evidence of those orations proves to a demonstration that the study and contemplation of the works of creation, and of the power and wisdom of God, revealed and manifested in those works, made a great part in the religious devotion of the times in which they were written; and it was this devotional study and contemplation that led to the discovery of the principles upon which what are now called sciences are established; and it is to the discovery of these*

> *principles that almost all the arts that contribute to the convenience of human life owe their existence. Every principal art has some science for its parent, though the person who mechanically performs the work does not always, and but very seldom, perceive the connection.* —The Age of Reason, Part 1, 1793

Thomas Paine wrote much more. One discussion, in particular, stands out when he wrote:

> *Of all the systems of religion that ever were invented, there is none more derogatory to the Almighty, more unedifying to man, more repugnant to reason, and more contradictory in itself, than this thing called Christianity. Too absurd for belief, too impossible to convince, and too inconsistent for practice, it renders the heart torpid, or produces only atheists and fanatics.* —The Age of Reason, Part 3, 1795

Understanding who or what the "Sun of God" is, is no longer an enigma. It may have been mysterious and difficult to understand for the ancients but should be understood by all in today's times. Perhaps you find the words *magic*, *mysterious*, and *blasphemous* to be inexplicably inexpressible. Go ahead and express them. Nothing is mysterious once you understand the workings. Nothing is magic when you establish how it was performed. And, finally, blasphemy becomes a state of your mind meaning "nothing."

Don't be inexpressible when you understand the workings. Today, we understand a thing or two because we have learned more than a thing or two.

We have come so far from the Homo sapiens munching bananas in a cave to this great leap in knowledge of astronomy, astrology, science, and technology. All anyone needs to do is read, and the truth will stare you in the face.

And even at that time, was Akhenaten's Aten—the Sun Disk—the first monotheistic attempt at a worship of a single star? You can now see that the answer is no. The practice had been before him. From Ra to Horus the practice rose to a new benchmark for Mithras, Krishna, and through other solar gods.

You can now see that the practice of the ancients is practically alive and well today. The practices may have been masked in various new religions, but all the markings—the DNA—of the original is present in the new.

This Earth is just as ordinary and almost insignificant when compared to the universe. As it is, Earth is infinitesimal in the mighty scheme of things, even though we think we are the center of the universe.

If you have read my book *Why Was Man Created?* you would have immediately understood how Homo sapiens are so new to the universe and significantly behind the curve in intelligence.

Our world is a creation of the software set in motion from the beginning. But some people are bent on making it seem more mysterious than the scientifically known facts because the majestically intriguing universe wows them.

I am also in awe, as you are.

They also want to keep the world's resources to a few. They, therefore, thought it wise to do something about it again around 2,000 years ago. So they made, borrowed, from the celestial environment and syncretized the characters they know little or nothing about. Those plans as we know now were diabolical.

Leaders had to have a story to explain why bad things happen to sinners in the afterlife. They created gods with edifying wowing characteristics. They then demanded you believe by faith in a period where reason, logic, and reality weren't a way of thinking.

So, the story about enduring tests of faith was born. They allegorized Satan too, who, if you have read this far, you already realized was the same as the Sun in the Most

## The Greatest Celestial Deception

High/Lowest Pit in the sky. Highest point being the heavens and hell the lowest point in a pit.

History tells us that the leaders went ahead and created stories so falsely pathetic, they bordered on cockamamy. Until recently, everybody seemed to have a need to be engorged with a belief. Beliefs which were, of course, created fabrications of outright disinformation, misinformation, or misinterpretations.

Many rich people around the world make their living talking about some random comments of nothings and sarcasm. In my, and perhaps your, neck of the woods, such talks are simply derided as blah-blah-blah.

But these people must find things to talk about, daily or weekly, especially with a crowd—congregants—gathered to listen. Most often, they speculate because speculating is the safest route where facts are not a hindrance.

The toughest part of this practice must be feigning wisdom and taking the job seriously. Perhaps their job is made simple by a crowd that can make use of true information, not misinformation. The irony here is that neither the "talker" nor the "listener" today has the correct information.

You see, in the very beginning, we were being disinformed, but today, we are being *mis*informed. Even if the agenda was disinformation because the people were ignorant and naïve back then, what is *our* excuse for the misinformation today? If the ancients had naïveté brought about by ignorance, what do *we* have?

The talking heads spreading the talking points from their books blab and encourage their listeners to put more money in the collection basket or check the donation box because in the name of the "Most High," they deserve a plane or two to reach more people.

Tell them next time that there is no Most High. There never was. There is the most high point in the heavens and the lowest point in the heavens. These two points were erroneously referred to as "heaven" and "hell."

Why does anyone even listen to a con artist? Perhaps it is that same lure—the wow factor—that lures people to a location where the con artist displays his/her practice.

Spirituality is a route to awareness and Oneness—an understanding—that all things are connected. It is quite different from religiosity.

Spirituality is about understanding, humanity, and knowledge, among other things, while religion is all about obedience to disinformation.

Spirituality is ever-present. Religion will someday, hopefully, be the past.

As religion salts and peppers its teachings with fear, what do you think would be human behavior when fear is taken out of the religion equation?

We are talking about fear as a weapon of control here. Sorry, my fellow human, hell was a creation of men, not a creation of the gods. Prophet Isaiah already told you so.

Most people worry that when the fear of hell is taken out of the religion equation, most people will start to do things that will ultimately destroy humanity. Really? Remind them of all the wars ever fought, most of which were fought because of religion and greed.

Are leaders of the world—most of whom are religious—not doing and caring less about humanity now? They get to power wearing religiosity on their sleeves, and soon after that, they transform into the nonexistent devil . . . or worse.

Your leaders know more than you think. They have access to the most important information. They are even privy to secret information they'd rather not discuss with you so that we can be easily manipulated. Some of them can be described as the proverbial "smart" ones leading the "ignorant" us. Put another way, they are the shepherds/herdsmen shepherding the sheep/cows. And religion is one of their best-weaponized tools.

The religions become antagonists of one another, even though they all derived their practices from one source, yet, individualizing and branding their practices differently.

The worries that a lack of religion would lead to unstable societies is unnecessary. Religion numbs the mind. Religion makes the mind stupid. Will a choice between stupidity or knowledge be easy to make?

Reasonable people don't think that way. Reasonable people know that the laws of the land are supreme and must be obeyed. Reasonable people know that you do not destroy the environment. Reasonable people do not depend on the control of religion to do the right thing. They do not engage in semantic satiation waiting for an unknown to solve known problems.

They just know and do the right things. They also know that all men are created equal, and all men must face, reasonably, the same benchmarks in most of our endeavors.

But a few men would never succumb to or do not want to subject themselves to the same benchmarks in all things. Religion, by its teachings, has hierarchies of a god, angels, monsters, and one angel who they called Satan.

And so, why must we castigate those men who want to be at the top? Have not the gods left us a legacy of servitude?

All the solar saviors are derivatives of the sun; hence, they all have familiar and similar characteristics.

## The Greatest Celestial Deception

Mention as many gods as you can remember from the ancients and they are derivatives of the sun.

However, the solar gods are not the same as angels and their leader. Angels, otherwise known as aliens, exist. While solar gods are allegories, aliens are real. Most of my books deal with alien stories.

If you have an urge to question some of the holy books, you won't be alone, but before you do that, bear in mind that the books contain a combination of stories written by various people from various eras.

Most of the problems emanate from misinterpretation, translation, and transliteration. Perhaps the biggest problem is the use of allegories, anthropomorphic, and religious motifs.

As a reader who is bent on making the "holy books" unravel for you and me, understanding the allegories and motifs and figuring the meaning behind their use illuminates the stories.

The manipulations of the books—the inputs, the removals, the outputs, the need for various versions with manipulated inputs, the disinformation and misinformation, where the interpretations were fantastic and the great job at cunningly conning its readers—were a marvel.

It was a bundle of well-crafted deception.

The disinformation took an even bigger step during the rewrite into other languages.

OK, before you go off suggesting that the Bible is the Word of God, how come there are variations in the editions of the various versions? How come the leaders of the times thought they had a free hand in manipulating the Bible? Was that not an assault on the sensibilities of ordinary people, even if they cannot question the king or the royalty?

That a king or royalty could manipulate the words in the Bible is reason enough to suggest that the books of the Bible are man-made, not inspired.

That they were manipulated makes the books no longer sacrosanct. Do you even believe that those "holy books" *were* sacrosanct?

For example:

If it were possible, an inquiry could have been made of the King James Version writers, translators, and reviewers for why they had things added or removed from the Bible while creating the King James Version. King James was human and historically existed. If they had reverence for Jesus so much as the Bible portrays, would they be altering what Jesus said and did not say?

One of the most iconic stories in the Bible was *added* centuries after the Bible was compiled. I love to christen that story: "Cast the first stone." It was the Pericope Adulterae from John 7:53; 8:1–11.

Here was a story that recorded a hero whose name was Jesus, who was full of compassion, courage, and conviction, standing up against the norms of the society and taking the side of an adulterer.

It was an amazing example of Jesus' defined sense of morality, but more importantly, a display of leadership. Most people quote John 8 as a reminder not to judge others. Jesus was described as writing on the ground, listening, and talking to the people with an adulterer standing in the middle. The gathered crowd asked for clarification from Jesus as they got ready to deliver justice. The penalty was Moses' injunction to put adulterers to death by stoning. You noticed that the man was not in the story. Does it not take two to tango?

Here too you observed that Jesus has been allegorized, humanized, and historicized, all at the same time.

Unfortunately, there is a very, very big problem with the above story. It did not happen.

The story was a forgery. It is still a forgery, and you may be wondering why that false story remains in the Bible. It was not biblical, but it is in the Bible.

Now, you see that the writers and reviewers of the Bible had long known that they could mess with the Bible as much as they wanted. You can even forge anything into . . . or out of . . . it. In those days (the 1500s), all you needed to do if you did not like a chapter or a verse in a story in the Bible, you sought and convinced a scholarly pawn of the "powerful" church to add whatever story you wanted in the next version of the Bible.

In fact, if you didn't like a whole book after the compilation at Nicaea, you could yank it out and add the ones you liked in your new version.

If a part of the Bible was false, what other parts were falsified? If the Bible can mislead in one instance, what degree of confidence do you have in its accuracy and authenticity?

If you study the story well, you can understand why there are very few scholars who believe this story of Jesus saving the helpless, adulterous woman to be authentic. There are many reasons. Firstly, you already know that Jesus did not exist. If anyone paraded themselves as Jesus, they borrowed the name.

Secondly, the story doesn't exist in the oldest, most "authentic" version of the Bible.

Thirdly, the style of writing does not fit or resemble the Gospel of John. The writing and language style was noticeably disconnected.

And finally, the story was suddenly and sloppily inserted into another story—the feast of the Tabernacles—which started from John 7:1 and was suddenly cut off so that the Pericope Adulterae was snuck in. The story of the Tabernacles finally resumes at John 8:12 to 9:7, and that is assuming you have the New Revised Standard Version of the Bible.

So, many questions arise.

Who added this story centuries later, and why? This story does not mention the name of the adulterous woman. Why, then, attribute this story to Mary Magdalene? What other parts of the Bible were added by scholarly pawns, and why? Why do most of the churches continue to teach this falsehood as truth and as a major story in the ministry of Jesus?

There are more questions, but let's diverge a bit.

The truth of the matter is: no lie will go unexposed. It is only a matter of time. The truth has a way of manifesting. Sometimes there is that wish and anticipation that we could have learned the truth sooner, but, hey, the situation is what it is.

What we now recognize was the historicism of celestial bodies into personalities in religions. And the allegories served as characters. The allegories of the solar gods as astrological amalgam were implicitly, yet explicitly, the copycatting of preceding gods.

Those who are good with histories can easily affirm for themselves that some past cultural practices were a carryover to present-day major religions. Some refer to those practices as paganism. If those were pagan practices, and Christianity borrowed from them, what, then, is Christian practice?

# The Greatest Celestial Deception

You have read about the sun god Ra and of Horus and all the characteristics they share with present-day allegory/characters used in today's popular religions.

On the walls of the temple in Luxor in present-day Egypt are images with the depiction of the Annunciation story line. It depicts the Immaculate Conception explicitly. Scene by scene, the depiction narrated the virgin birth and of the adoration of "young" Horus.

The Nativity Scene depicted on the Luxor Temple at about 1500 BC, about 3,500 years ago, on the walls also depicts Thoth announcing to the Virgin Isis that she will conceive and bear a child—Horus, with Kneph, the "Holy Ghost," impregnating the virgin, and of the infant being visited by three kings/magi bearing gifts.

Have you not heard this story before, my dear reader?

If you compare the stories of the solar gods, including Jesus, you will see that there are no differences in the whole concept. The solar gods, especially Jesus, were a psychological tool in a fight for the control of mankind from Rome and the territories they occupied around the Mediterranean and every other region where they had their form of a solar god.

Put another way, the idea of Jesus and other celestial gods was just the way smart ancient people controlled the ignorant ones.

And it still works today.

# The Greatest Celestial Deception

If you compare just Horus and Jesus, both were the same stories told at different times. Therefore, one of the stories must be the original and the other the counterfeit. One, therefore, must have borrowed from the original.

Does the above story from the depiction on the wall in Egypt ring a bell with you?

If it does not, perhaps the same words from Thomas Paine we used earlier in the beginning pages will boldly spell it out and will now be better understood:

*The Christian religion is a parody on the worship of the Sun, in which they put a man whom they call Christ, in the place of the Sun, and pay him the same adoration which was originally paid to the Sun.*

Thomas Paine wasn't done. He went on to say, perhaps sarcastically:

> *If Jesus Christ was the being which those Mythologists tell us he was, and that he came into this world to suffer, which is a word they sometimes use instead of to die, the only real suffering he could have endured, would have been to live. His existence here was a state of exilement or transportation from Heaven, and the way back to his original country was to die. In fine,*

> *everything in this strange system is
> the reverse of what it pretends to be.*

Jesus, like all other solar gods, was an allegory. "He" came into existence by being anthropomorphized and simply historicized. But the official position right this moment and in the nearest future will be: Deny. Deny. Deny.

Consciousness—the Intelligent Creator—cannot be crucified. Only man can be crucified. What sense does it make to you that the Creator of multiverses, each with many thousands of light-years in size, would come to this insignificantly infinitesimal Earth after many billions of years after or during creation, only to be crucified by some intelligence-challenged humanoids? We cannot even crucify the sun.

Religion is a tragedy for all involved—it is like you were wrongfully deprived of your liberties during the prime of your life following a religion you thought you understood. This time can never be returned to you, but with today's enlightenment, we hope you can begin the process of unburdening and, perhaps, giving you a new chance at a truth that brightens a successful future.


Let us hope that inquisitiveness, education, and learning will be the weapons that bring this entire Legoland of religions crashing down on themselves, so that we will no longer feel like hell is living on earth with religion.

# The Greatest Celestial Deception

If you are downtrodden or even in power, your first best response is to cut out the fears. Learn and understand what or where the fear is coming from and cut it out. We are the answer to our fears and problems.

Finally, all of us in this world are the answers to our own fears and problems. We can always harness nature to solve our many problems. It is, after all, one life to live. Don't waste part of it on existing but anthropomorphized celestial bodies while succumbing to the fears. It is time to start living before you stop living.

The End

Below are a few of my other books. You or your friends might like one of them. A reasonable review will be appreciated too. I thank you in advance if you decide to do a review.

1. Why Was Man Created?
   https://www.amazon.com/dp/B00G5FDJKC

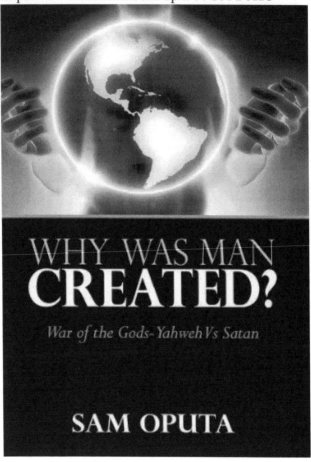

2. Faith or Reason
   https://www.amazon.com/dp/1478733179

3. Akashic Records or Free Will . . .
   https://www.amazon.com/dp/1548253464

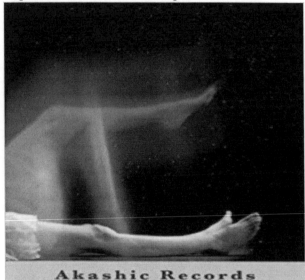

# Bibliography

Lee Felicia R. (2003). *From Noah's Curse to Slavery's Rationale:* Retrieved from http://www.nytimes.com/2003/11/01/arts/from-noah-s-curse-to-slavery-s-rationale.html

GNU Free license. (2002). Retrieved from http://www.fact-index.com/j/je/jewish_eschatology.html

Bible Quotes are from NRSV. Retrieved from www.biblegateway.com/

Bible Quotes also from KJV. Retrieved from www.biblegateway.com/

Paine, Thomas. (1793) *The Age of Reason*, Part 1. Retrieved from http://www.revolutionary-war-and-beyound.com/quotes-by-thomas-paine.html

Paine, Thomas. (1795) The Age of Reason, Part 3. Retrieved from http://www.revolutionary-war-and-beyound.com/quotes-by-thomas-paine.html

# The Greatest Celestial Deception

Printed in Poland
by Amazon Fulfillment
Poland Sp. z o.o., Wrocław